MINIATURE
DESSERTS

BOOK PURCHASED
Miniature Desserts
PLACE Barts
DATE 1-2003   AMOUNT 3,50
COMMENTS

Carol Geisert

BOOK PURCHASED
Miniature Desserts
PLACE Barts
DATE 1-2003   AMOUNT 3,50
COMMENTS

MINIATURE DESSERTS

PAM DOTTER

WEIDENFELD & NICOLSON
New York

Published by Weidenfeld & Nicolson, New York
A Division of Wheatland Corporation
10 East 53rd Street
New York, NY 10022

Created and produced by Phoebe Phillips Editions

Library of Congress Cataloging-in-Publication Data

Dotter, Pam.
  Miniature desserts.

  Includes index.
  1. Desserts.   I. Title.
TX773.D68   1986   641.8′6   86-11000
ISBN 1-55584-013-2

Designed by Rachael Foster and Anthony Short
Phototypeset in Garamond ITC by Bookworm Typesetting, Manchester
Printed and Bound in Italy by Sagdos

First Edition 1986

10 9 8 7 6 5 4 3 2 1

My thanks to the following for the help I have received in writing this book: my husband Frank who encouraged and tasted, Jacqui Hine who helped me develop and test the recipes then prepared the desserts so beautifully for photography, and Lynda Tyler and Joyce Weston for their help in typing the manuscript.

Contents

Introduction

The delicious, delectable desserts in this book are as good to look at as they are to eat, and can be combined to create a magical effect of light and color on your table.

They reflect a new kind of cooking, for the very newest kind of dining. Today, no one wants to get up from a dinner table loaded down with excess cream and satiated with the over-rich taste of too much sweetness. People have learned to eat well, and lightly. They appreciate that the subtle flavors and delicate charms of fine desserts are best enjoyed in small quantities. In the best of the new restaurants, too, clever *maîtres d'hôtel* suggest a mouthful of this and a tiny swirl of that, instead of heaping customers' plates with gargantuan slices of layer cake.

At home we do our guests an injury by expecting them to overeat, especially of the deliciously sweet desserts most people love. But a single tiny tart can be the perfect ending to a meal, as can a bite of apple crumble, a spoonful of lemon soufflé, a single fresh berry in a coating of richest chocolate.

A guest need not feel awkward refusing dessert, nor a hostess mortified because no one touches her dish of fruit fritters. Turn those fritters from thick slices of pineapple coated in batter, into individual mouthfuls – even a layer cake into tiny jeweled squares – and both guest and hostess will be happy.

With desserts created in miniature there is no need to stint on using the finest ingredients available, and the recipes that follow use light cream whips, exotic liqueurs, the tiniest of new fruits, smooth butters and chocolates, crisp pastries, melting chestnut purées and glistening crystallized fruits. Why not, when so little is required for each portion?

But there are also new ways of serving simple traditional favorites: Christmas puddings so small that their holly leaf decoration almost covers them; tiny golden sponge desserts; minute squares of glowing wine gelatins; slivers of cheesecake.

Although these tend to be for more formal, festive occasions, other recipes in *Miniature Desserts* are just right for an informal dinner party with friends – what could be better than a choice of seasonal fruits, each berry or slice dipped in white and dark chocolate? The recipes are also useful for family meals: instead of baking huge cakes, adapt a basic sponge cake recipe to make a variety of tiny morsels or a selection of tartlets and pies from a single pastry recipe.

This introduction is followed by a chapter on making and serving miniature desserts, with ideas for suitable containers and other equipment and suggestions on how to combine and serve different kinds of dishes.

The chapters that follow are divided according to type of dessert – molded, iced, cakes or cookies, for instance – and, often, the main ingredient used – egg white in Meringues and Macaroons, for example, cream in Cream Desserts. Most chapters in the book are further subdivided into various categories.

Molded Desserts, for example, consists of cheesecakes, wine gelatins and soufflés and mousses. And each category starts with a basic recipe highlighted in a tinted box. In turn, each of these recipes can be adapted to allow you to produce a range of variations on the basic theme.

Quantities for these basic recipes vary, according to what is practical. It is easier, for example, to handle a small amount of batter than the same amount of gelatin mixture which will set before you have time to divide it into individual portions. Many of the variations call for half, or even quarter, quantities of the basic recipe. In other cases, especially when an ingredient is replaced during making, each variation requires the "full" amount of the basic recipe.

Remember, though, that one of the greatest advantages of these miniature desserts is that the basic recipes can be multiplied, as well as divided, to give three or four parts that can be flavored and shaped to produce from four to eight portions of three or four different desserts. If you freeze any left over after a dinner party, you will soon have a selection of miniature desserts to offer guests.

The number and size of portions that each recipe will yield is given in **bold type** above the list of ingredients. Remember though that these are miniature desserts, so a portion is by no means all anyone can eat – unless he or she is on a highly restricted diet.

Three or four portions should be enough for most people, but obviously, if your guests are hearty eaters, they will be tempted to try even more delicious recipes. If anyone is trying very hard to keep their calorie intake to a minimum, one perfect – but tiny – dessert will allow them a touch of luxury at the end of their meal, and still leave them feeling virtuous.

Ingredients for a number of desserts include items like icing, butter creams, custard, etc. Recipes for all these are highlighted with an asterisk, and given in detail in Creating Miniature Desserts, from page 147. If a "made up" ingredient is a recipe in one of the main chapters, we give the page number.

Appearance is all-important when serving these tiny desserts, and ingredients include finishing touches like marzipan or chocolate leaves, frosted petals and other delights. These are also highlighted with an asterisk, and, like icings, etc are given in full in Creating Miniature Desserts. In both cases, check with the index for exact page numbers if necessary.

Remember that cooking times may change slightly. The weather affects how quickly a gelatin or a soufflé sets, the range of heat in your oven may vary when you are dealing with very small quantities of pastry, and microwave ovens must be used according to their instructions.

Making Miniature Desserts

Think small – in every way – if you want to succeed at creating, and making, miniature desserts. Start with unusual uses for standard kitchen equipment, and continue through practical matters like adapting freezing and storage methods for tiny quantities, to the most enjoyable aspect of this latest way of entertaining: combining different desserts to suit every occasion and every possible taste.

Equipment

All kinds of gadgets and kitchen equipment are available to make your task carefree and straightforward, and many utensils can be adapted to help you get professional results.

Preparation

Assemble your ingredients on plates before you begin cooking, so that you can see exactly what you have. If you do this, small quantities of spices and flavorings will not get lost.

Measuring spoons, from ¼ teaspoon capacity to a tablespoon are a necessity, as are small wooden spoons. Use small plastic spoons to crush soft fruits lightly without absorbing the juice or the colorings.

Tea cups, or even egg cups, can be used for mixing small quantities.

A few small strainers, like the ones used for straining coffee, are useful for puréeing ingredients and sprinkling powdered sugar. It is often – but not always – quicker and easier to strain than blend in your normal electric machinery. Of course, if the quantity is large enough, and certainly if you are preparing for a large party, processors and electric blenders will be ideal.

When buying baking equipment, look at gadgets made for confectioners, and for making petits fours, available from specialist kitchenware shops.

Tiny molds, in decorative shapes, are perfect for tartlets and puddings; aspic cutters are smaller than normal cookie ones; or investigate the pleasant and unusual shapes available from stores' baking departments.

Learn to look searchingly at the most unlikely sources. Bottle caps make round shapes in a wide variety of sizes; large embroidery needles can be used to prick designs in miniature pie crusts; china

sake cups hold tiny puddings for steaming – set them into small bamboo steamers, normally used for *dim sum*, Chinese dumplings.

Although most baking pans and molds are too large for individual desserts, use the smallest tart size, usually about 4in, to make a single tart that can be divided into four or even six portions.

Mold cheesecakes in miniature bread pans, before slicing them. Half-filled, the pans are good containers for bar cakes, which can be sliced into thin portions.

Small yogurt containers are ideal for molding individual soufflés and gâteaux. Use baby food cans, open at one end, for steaming puddings or for setting gelatins or other molded desserts.

Choose small star piping tubes – the kind made for icing are ideal – for soft cookie mixtures and eclairs.

Use small aluminum foil plates for pie crusts, and put them on a baking sheet so that they have some support in the oven.

If you cannot find any small cups for steaming, use egg cups instead. If you are handy with a pair of scissors, it is simple to cut through the side of a foil or waxed paper cup, overlap the sides so that the inside is much smaller, and then tape the outside together with masking tape. Crumple a little foil in a large cup to support this smaller version.

Use double thickness of heavy foil to mold containers of all shapes.

Serving

A selection of dolls' house furniture – tiny tables and sideboards, for example – makes delightful platters on which to serve one or two desserts.

Demitasse cups, in the very smallest size, are ideal containers for ladies' fingers. The saucers are usually both decorative and tiny; with a doily in the middle to disguise the indentation, they are perfect small plates. Coasters can also double as plates.

Little silver salt cellars can be called into use for glamorous dinner parties; use china versions for more informal family meals.

Use doilies to cover the center holes in the glass and crystal bobèches that were set into candlesticks to keep the wax from dripping onto the table, and put a slice of cake on top of each.

Use melon ball scoops for ice creams and gelatins. The small end of a double-sided scoop is ideal for fresh fruits.

Paper cases made for chocolates and petits fours will hold tartlets or slices of cake, and can also be used as molds for chocolate cases.

Make foaming mousse desserts in the smallest available liqueur glasses instead of wine goblets, and use tiny sugar spoons for eating.

Serve tiny scoops of ice cream or sorbet in sherry glasses.

Planning Ahead

It makes good sense to have a selection of tiny desserts, or basic preparations
like crusts and edible containers, ready to use.

Storage

Many of the basic recipes in the following chapters can be used to make different flavored desserts, and freezing any that remain after a dinner party is a simple way to keep some for future use. Or put aside a few hours now and then to stock up your freezer; prepare the recipes to a stage where you will only need to add a few fresh ingredients and decorations to have desserts for any occasion.

Remember that tiny quantities freeze – and thaw – very quickly. If any of the larger gâteaux or desserts are to be divided, slice them while they are still half-frozen. Dessert "basics" like cakes, crusts, crêpes and waffles can be made ahead in quantity, and frozen before they are filled or decorated. Choux pastry can be filled with whipped cream before freezing, although it will lose a little of its crispness.

Put sheets of waxed paper between individual items so that they can be easily separated when you take them out of the freezer.

To freeze small, decorated cakes, simply stand them on a metal tray and let them get really hard before wrapping and labeling them.

Gelatins and gelatin mixtures do not usually freeze very well – clear gelatins collapse on thawing – but foamy mousses and soufflés can be frozen quite successfully if they are left in their original containers.

Cookies, meringues and macaroons can be stored for up to six weeks in a closed box, provided it is really airtight. Use your freezer for longer storage

Fruit cakes store very well for comparatively long periods, but remember to keep them moist – small sizes dry out quickly. A teaspoon of brandy added every week or so will do the trick.

Make fillings and creams ahead of time and store them separately in the freezer. Decorative marzipan flowers, cut candied fruit peel and toasted nuts can be made in large quantities and stored in airtight boxes.

Creative Combinations

Different desserts can be combined in all kinds of ways to match a variety of tastes and occasions. These are only a few suggestions.

French style A slither of Tarte Française, a taste of Meringue Belle Hélène, followed by Normandy Flan and Crème à la Coeur.

Crisp and crunchy Bite into Chocolate Cheesecake and tiny Ginger Nuggets, serve with Crunchnut Torten and Apple Crumble puddings.

Bittersweet delights Enjoy the contrast of Chocolate and Orange Roulade, Raspberries au Fromage and Coconut and Cheese Snaps.

Colorful berries Arrange Ripe Berry Tartlets with bright Spiced Blackberry and Apple Kissel, Blueberry Tarts, Red Berry Yogurt Ice Cream and elegant Red Currant Lilies.

Exotic fruits A scoop of Passion Fruit Water Ice, a dip into Banana and Rum Moscovite, a succulent spoonful of chilled Mango Soufflé, a portion of Glacé Fruit Bombe and a last lingering taste of Peach Melba.

Desserts for all seasons Conjure up New Year's Day with Athol Brose and festive Pecan Pie; round off the winter with Cherry Ripe Tartlets and Valentine Pavlovas; make delectable spring desserts of Peaches and Praline Cream mini-crêpes, Citrus Fruit Salad and Smooth Cheesecake Pie; celebrate summer with Rose Cream Meringues, and enter into the autumn spirit with St Clement's Creams and Golden Fruit Kissel.

Autumn harmony Blend the colors of Chocolate Chestnut Meringues with Chilled Ginger Soufflé, Walnut Coffee Tartlets with Flambéed Apricots, and contrast golden Syrup Puddings with Coffee Liqueur Granita.

Mid-summer surprise A taste of Chilled Zabaglione followed by Tropical Fruit Salad, traditional Summer Pudding, cool Pina Colada Ice Cream, Rich Secret Desserts and refreshing Lemon Water Ice.

Eastern promise Taste the East with tangy Ginger and Yogurt Moscovite, Maraschino Pyramid and Eastern Pearls; serve with Mango Slices, Harlequin Mallows, Tropical Surprises and Cinnamon-flavoured Danish Pastries.

Spring fever Get in the mood with Cherry Blossom Cheesecakes, Champagne Hearts, Rainbow Profiteroles, Apricot Pavlovas, Cinnamon Flowers and Green Fruit Salad.

Apples and pears Brandied Apple Fritters, Flambéed Pears, Apple and Raisin Danish Pastry, Pears with Gin and Lime Juice and Spiced Apple Crescents.

High spirits Kick off with Liqueur Barrels, Chestnut and Rum Ice Cream, Honey and Rum Babas and end with Tipsy Peaches. Serve with Brandy Snaps.

Molded Desserts

These beautifully shaped desserts range from clear, sparkling wine gelatins set with fruits to fluffy creams, and shaped morsels and balls piled high in glasses. There are also tiny soufflés set in chocolate cups, delicate fruit mousses and creamy chilled cheesecakes.

Chilled Cheesecakes

Chilled, gelatin-based cheesecakes can be molded and flavored with fruit, chocolate and even chestnuts. They can be made creamy with full-fat soft cheese or less rich with cottage or other low-fat cheeses. Use the basic chilled cheesecake recipe to make all the delicious desserts that follow.

Chilled Cheesecake

Two 4 × 4in cheesecakes: 16 portions

For the bases
Two square 4in Golden Crumb Crust bases (page 41)

Filling
1 tablespoon powdered gelatin
8 tablespoons full-fat cream cheese
1 egg yolk
Grated rind of half a lemon
2 tablespoons sugar
1/2–3/4 cup sour or heavy cream

Place Golden Crumb Crust bases on a double thickness of foil large enough to extend 1in up each side to form a box. Fold corners to neaten and secure.
    Place gelatin in 3 tablespoons cold water in a small bowl. Place bowl over a pan of hot water or in a microwave oven for 1/2 minute to melt gelatin.
    Place cream cheese, egg yolk, lemon rind and sugar in a medium bowl and beat until smooth. Gradually beat in the cream and the melted gelatin. Divide the mixture in half and flavor as in the recipes that follow.
    Pour the mixture onto prepared crusts, level tops and chill until set. Carefully remove foil, gently running a hot knife between cheesecake and foil if necessary. Place cheesecakes on serving plates and decorate as desired.

Orange and Chocolate Cheesecake

One 4 × 4in cheesecake; 8 portions

2 teaspoons finely grated orange rind
1 tablespoon orange juice
Orange food coloring
1 tablespoon finely chopped semi-sweet chocolate
1/2 Chilled Cheesecake mixture
One square 4in Golden Crumb Crust base (page 41)

Decoration
4 squares chocolate, melted
3 tablespoons whipped cream
8 Glazed Kumquat Slices*

Fold orange rind, juice, one or two drops of orange food coloring and the chocolate into the cheesecake mixture. Pour onto crust, prepared as for Chilled Cheesecake, and level top. Chill to set.
    Remove foil.
    To decorate, place melted chocolate into a waxed paper icing bag and drizzle chocolate over top of cheesecake. Pipe eight small rosettes of cream on the cheesecake and position a Glazed Kumquat Slice on top of each.

Previous pages, clockwise from left *Harlequin Mallow (page 25); 3in Red Currant Lily (page 24) surrounded by Chocolate Chestnut Meringues (opposite); Black Currant and Litchi Ring (page 20).*

Chocolate and Almond Cheesecake Gâteau

One 3 × 4in gâteau; 6 portions

2 ounces semi-sweet chocolate
1/2 Chilled Cheesecake mixture, omitting gelatin
18 tiny macaroons
3 tablespoons rum or sherry

Decoration
2 tablespoons whipped cream
6 black cherries or grapes

Melt chocolate in a small bowl over hot water. Stir into cheesecake mixture. Dip the macaroons in the rum or sherry for 30 seconds on each side.

Place a 4in wide by 6in long strip of waxed paper into a 3 × 4in container to extend up the sides at either end for easy removal. Place six macaroons in the base and spread with half the mixture. Repeat with macaroons and mixture ending with a layer of macaroons. Cover and leave in the refrigerator overnight.

Lift out of mold, remove paper and place on a serving plate. Pipe a rosette of cream on each macaroon and place a cherry or grape on top. To serve, cut into six slices.

Chocolate Chestnut Meringues

Eight 2½in meringues

3 tablespoons sweetened chestnut purée
1 Chilled Cheesecake mixture, using half the quantity of gelatin and omitting the egg yolk

Decoration
16 Mini Meringue Shells (page 122)
4 ounces chocolate, melted

Place a 1in wide strip of waxed paper inside eight ¼ cup barrel-shaped molds.

Beat the chestnut purée until smooth then fold into the cheesecake mixture. Divide the mixture between the molds and leave to set.

Unmold the cheesecakes by inverting the mold and shaking each over a plate. Remove the paper. Place a Mini Meringue Shell at each end of every cheesecake and pipe chocolate across the top of each one.

Cherry Blossom Cheesecakes

Six 1½in cheesecakes

1/4 cup maraschino cherries
1/2 Chilled Cheesecake mixture
1½ tablespoons maraschino syrup from the jar or can

Decoration
3/4–1 cup Green Marzipan*
Powdered sugar
6 small ginger snaps about 1½in in diameter
2 tablespoons kirsch
1 tablespoon chopped pistachio nuts

Finely chop cherries and fold into cheesecake mixture with syrup. Divide mixture between six 3 tablespoon pots or egg cups. Leave to set.

Roll out marzipan and trim to 4 × 14in. Cut down its length into three 1¼in strips, then cut twelve 1¼in leaf shapes diagonally from each strip, six for each serving. Sprinkle six individual tartlet pans of 2 tablespoon capacity with powdered sugar, then press the leaves, slightly overlapping, into each. Leave several hours or until the marzipan has set, then carefully remove from pans and leave to dry overnight.

Soak the cookies in the kirsch for 30 seconds both sides then place one in each marzipan leaf case. Unmold cheesecakes and position one on top of each cookie. Sprinkle pistachio nuts on top of each cheesecake to represent stamens.

> **A firmer cheesecake**
> Cheesecakes may also be made with cottage cheese which will give a slightly drier texture.

Wine Gelatins

Wine gelatins are remarkable for their adaptability and their delicate flavor. They can be used plain, flavored or mixed with fruit, and molded to almost any shape that strikes your fancy. Instead of white wine a rosé gives a delightful effect. If you use a dark or tawny dessert wine, on the other hand, fruit and purées will not show up so well, as the color will be changed.

Wine Gelatin

6 portions

1⅛ cup sweet white wine
2 tablespoons sugar
1 tablespoon lemon juice
1 tablespoon powdered gelatin

Place wine, sugar and lemon juice in a scrupulously clean small saucepan and gently warm the mixture. Remove from heat, sprinkle in the gelatin, and leave 2 minutes to soften. Then stir over a low heat until the gelatin has dissolved. Do not boil. Strain into a measuring cup and leave to cool.
Use before setting point and flavor as required.

Cream Gelatin

6 portions

Beat 6 tablespoons full-fat cream cheese with 2 tablespoons of the Wine Gelatin until smooth. Beat in remaining gelatin.

Black Currant Gelatin

6 portions

Add 3 tablespoons black currant syrup or Crème de Cassis liqueur to the Wine Gelatin.

Jellied Fruit Salad

Six ¼ cup gelatins

1 unset Wine Gelatin
1 kiwi fruit
¼ cup wild strawberries (or small firm strawberries)

Decoration
Chantilly Cream (page 122)
6 wild (or small) strawberries with stalks

Set a little Wine Gelatin in the bases of six ¼ cup molds. Peel and slice kiwi fruit and cut slices into four or six pieces. Halve strawberries (or quarter if strawberries are larger). Layer a little fruit with a little gelatin in the molds, setting each layer in a cool place before adding the next. When the molds are full leave to set firmly.
Dip the molds in hand-hot water and invert onto cold plates.
Pipe a rosette of Chantilly Cream on top of each one and decorate with a strawberry. Use the day it is made.

A firm gelatin
Never allow the gelatin to boil or you will spoil its setting quality.

Left *Maraschino Pyramid (page 20) served in a liqueur glass.*

Maraschino Pyramid

Six ¼ cup pyramids

¼ cup maraschino cherries
1 unset Cream Gelatin, as recipe (page 19)
1 tablespoon sugar

Decoration
¼ cup maraschino cherries
2 tablespoons maraschino syrup

Finely chop ¼ cup cherries and stir into unset Cream Gelatin with the sugar. Pour into a small, deep container and leave to set.

To make the sauce, blend the cherries with the syrup in an electric blender, then press the purée through a nylon strainer.

Form the set gelatin into balls with a warmed melon baller, place on a metal tray and chill until firm. (Melt the remaining gelatin over warm water and repeat.)

To serve, stack the balls in pyramids in six tiny bowl-shaped glasses and trickle the sauce over them.

Black Currant and Litchi Rings

Six 1½ in rings

1 unset Black Currant Gelatin, as recipe (page 19)
¾ cup fresh or ½ cup canned litchis

Decoration
Frosted Mint Leaves*

Pour gelatin into six ¼ cup ring molds and chill until set. Peel litchis and remove the pits. Chop half the fruit and reserve for decoration. Blend remaining fruit in an electric blender.

To serve, dip molds in hand-hot water, invert onto six small chilled plates. Fill the centers with chopped litchis and decorate with Frosted Mint Leaves. Pour a little litchi sauce around each and chill until ready to serve.

Eastern Pearls

Six ¼ cup portions

1⅛ cup skimmed milk
1 tablespoon powdered gelatin
Flavoring (see below)

Decoration
6 fresh mango slices
6 kiwi fruit slices
2 tablespoons chopped pistachio nuts

Place the milk in a scrupulously clean small saucepan and warm gently. Remove from the heat, sprinkle in the gelatin, and leave 2 minutes to soften. Then stir over a low heat until the gelatin has dissolved. Do not boil. Strain into a measuring cup and leave to cool. Place a flavoring and coloring in three small bowls and add one-third of the milk gelatin to each. Pour into three rectangular plastic containers about 4 × 5in and chill until set.

Cut gelatin into small squares in each container and invert each onto wetted waxed paper; tap the bottom of the containers to release the gelatin.

Arrange mixed cubes in six bowl-shaped sherry glasses with the mango and kiwi fruit slices. Sprinkle with pistachio nuts.

Almond
A few drops almond extract and a drop of green food coloring.

Rose
A few drops of rose water and a drop of pink food coloring.

Coffee
½ teaspoon instant coffee dissolved in 1 teaspoon boiling water.

How to chop gelatin
Place gelatin on wetted waxed paper on a chopping board. Use a hot or wet knife to chop the gelatin.

Soufflés and Mousses

Egg whites add air to soufflés, while mousses are lightened with whipped cream. Both can be flavored and shaped in all kinds of ways. The recipes that follow include soufflés in chocolate cases, and variations on fruit-based mousses. Take care to fold the flavorings in gently using a metal spoon to avoid spoiling the delicate texture.

Chilled Soufflé

6 portions

2 teaspoons powdered gelatin
1 teaspoon grated lemon rind
2 eggs, separated
3 level tablespoons sugar
3/8 cup heavy cream

Place gelatin with 2 tablespoons cold water in a small bowl and dissolve over a pan of hot water, or in a microwave oven. Leave to cool.

Place lemon rind, egg yolks and sugar (together with flavor as below) in a bowl over hot water and beat until mixture is thick and creamy. Remove from heat and beat until cool. Beat in gelatin.

Whip egg whites and cream separately until they just hold their shape, then fold them into the mixture. Pour into containers and leave to set.

Vanilla
Beat in 1 teaspoon vanilla extract or use Vanilla Sugar*.

Chocolate
Melt 2 ounces semi-sweet chocolate in a small bowl over hot water, and beat in with the egg yolks.

Lemon
Beat in the grated rind and juice of 1 lemon with the egg yolks. For lemon tang soufflé replace the cream with sour cream or natural yogurt.

Orange
Beat in the grated rind and juice of half an orange (small), and 1 tablespoon lemon juice. Tint pale orange with food coloring.

Lime
Beat in the grated rind and juice of 1 lime and half a lemon. Tint pale green with food coloring.

Ginger
Chop 6 pieces of preserved ginger and fold in with 1 tablespoon ginger syrup from the jar.

Apricot
Make apricot purée by blending canned or cooked fresh apricots in an electric blender. Add 1/2–3/4 cup to soufflé mixture with the egg yolks.

Mango
As apricot, using peeled strained mangoes.

Ingredients, sauces, edible containers, etc that are asterisked in the recipes on these pages are given in detail on pages 147 to 156. For exact page numbers, refer to the index at the end of the book.

Lime Charlottes

Six ¼ cup charlottes

1 Chilled Soufflé mixture with lime flavor (page 21)

Decoration
36 coffee-flavored "matchsticks"
¼ cup Chantilly Cream (page 122)
1½ slices of fresh lime
2 yards narrow green ribbon

Pour soufflé into six ¼ cup dariole molds or straight-sided round plastic molds. Leave to set. Turn molds out onto cold plates.

Cut matchsticks to height of molds and press around the sides to cover. Tie a piece of ribbon around each charlotte. Pipe small rosettes of Chantilly Cream around the top edges of the soufflés and decorate with small pieces of lime.

Mango Slices

Two ½ cup soufflés; 12 slices

1 Chilled Mango Soufflé mixture (page 21) using 2 teaspoons honey instead of sugar
Replace the whipped cream in the basic mixture with ½ cup natural yogurt
4 tablespoons mango purée

Decoration
1 teaspoon powdered gelatin
A few pieces of very thinly sliced mango

To make the decoration, first place the gelatin in 2 tablespoons cold water in a small bowl. Melt over a pan of hot water or in a microwave oven. Spoon a little into the bases of two ½ cup oblong containers such as metal bread pans. Leave to set then arrange mango pieces on it. Cover with a thin layer of the gelatin and leave to set.

Spoon soufflé mixture into prepared molds. Leave to set. Turn molds out onto a cold plate and chill before slicing.

Serve two slices for each portion on chilled plates. Decorate with mango pieces.

Cup Soufflés

Six ¼ cup soufflés

6 Chocolate Cases*, using small paper cake cases
1 Chilled Soufflé mixture (page 21)

Prepare the "cups" before making the soufflé.

Place a 1in wide piece of double foil around the top edge of each Chocolate Case to make a "collar" above the case. Make a little fold to secure. Fill with soufflé mixture and chill until set. Carefully remove the collars by running a hot knife between the foil and soufflé.

Lemon Cup Soufflés

Six ¼ cup soufflés

1 Chilled Soufflé mixture with lemon flavor (page 21)
6 Chocolate Cases*

Decoration
2 tablespoons whipped cream
Pinch of Glazed Lemon Peel Strands*
1 slice lemon

Make Cup Soufflés as described in previous recipe.

Remove foil and decorate with lemon strands. Cut the lemon slice in half and arrange on the plate.

Lime or Orange Cup Soufflés

Replace lemon flavor Chilled Soufflé mixture with lime or orange flavor (page 21), and replace lemon slice and strands with lime or orange slices and strands.

Ginger Cup Soufflé

Six ¼ cup soufflés

6 Chocolate Cases*
1 Chilled Soufflé with ginger flavor (page 21)

Decoration
2 tablespoons whipped cream
6 slices preserved ginger
24 piped Chocolate Shapes*

Make up Cup Soufflés as described, and remove foil collars.

Decorate with piped cream, ginger slices and Chocolate Shapes.

Right, from top *¼ cup Lemon, Lime and Orange Cup Soufflés (opposite).*

Fruit Mousse

6 portions

2 teaspoons powdered gelatin
½–¾ cup fruit purée
2 teaspoons lemon juice
¾ cup whipping cream

Place gelatin with 3 tablespoons cold water in a small bowl. Melt over a pan of hot water or in a microwave oven. Leave to cool; then stir into fruit purée with lemon juice.

Whip cream until it just holds its shape and fold it into the fruit purée. Pour into mold and leave to set.

Dip mold in hand-hot water and invert onto a chilled plate.

Red Currant Lilies

Six 3 × 3in lilies

½lb red currants
1 unset Fruit Mousse mixture

Decoration
6 ounces filo pastry
2 tablespoons sugar
Small bunches of Frosted Red Currants (page 97)

Cook red currants in ⅝ cup water in a covered saucepan over a low heat until soft. Drain, reserving juice, then strain fruit. Stir purée into mousse mixture. Divide the mixture between six ¼ cup molds and leave to set.

Heat the oven to 375°F. Grease the outside of six over-turned ovenproof cups. Cut the filo pastry into 18 squares of 4 × 4in and drape three squares loosely over each cup without letting the pastry stick to the sides. Bake 10 to 12 minutes until crisp and golden. Leave to cool then carefully remove from cups.

Dissolve sugar in ⅝ cup red currant juice over a medium heat then bring to a boil and continue boiling until juice is reduced by half. Cool.

Unmold red currant mousses and place one in each pastry case. Drizzle a little sauce over them and place a bunch of Frosted Red Currants on each case.

Chocolate-Centered Chestnut Mousses

Six ¼ cup mousses

1 unset Fruit Mousse mixture, made with 4
*   tablespoons sweetened chestnut purée and juice*
*   of ½ orange instead of fruit purée*
2 ounces semi-sweet chocolate
2 teaspoons dark rum

Decoration
2 tablespoons sweetened chestnut purée
6 maraschino cherries

Using half the chestnut mousse mixture, divide between six ¼ cup deep molds or tiny after-dinner coffee cups.

Melt the chocolate in a small bowl over a pan of hot water. Stir into remaining chestnut mousse, with the rum. Place the mixture into a nylon piping bag with a large plain tube and pipe it into the centers of the molds. Leave to set.

With a small tube, pipe sweetened chestnut purée in ribbons onto serving plates making six circles slightly larger than the molds. Dip the molds into hand-hot water; invert one in the center of each chestnut ring. Place a cherry on each.

To unmold mousses and soufflés
Loosen edge of mold with fingertips and dip mold into a bowl of hand-hot water. Take it out almost immediately and place a plate over the mold, then invert mold and plate and shake gently. When dessert has been released, carefully remove mold to avoid damaging the surface.

Gooseberry Mousses

Six ¼ cup mousses

Green food coloring
1 unset Fruit Mousse mixture made with gooseberry
* purée*

Decoration
6 Macaroon Fingers (page 129)
⅝ cup light cream

Stir a little food coloring into the mousse and set the mixture in six ¼ cup popsicle molds.

Unmold onto cold plates and place a Macaroon Finger into each one to represent a stick. Serve with cream.

Harlequin Mallows

Eight ¼ cup mallows

8 white marshmallows
4 red glacé cherries
2 green glacé cherries
1 unset Fruit Mousse made with ⅝ cup apple purée

Decoration
5 pink marshmallows
3 tablespoons pale dry sherry
6 tablespoons heavy cream, whipped
Pink food coloring
*Pink Chocolate Butterflies**

Snip the marshmallows into small pieces with wetted scissors. Chop the red and green cherries and fold into the mousse with the marshmallows. Divide mixture between eight ¼ cup molds or cups and leave to set in the refrigerator.

Place the pink marshmallows and sherry in a small bowl and melt over hot water or in a microwave oven. Fold into the whipped cream and tint pink with food coloring.

To serve, dip molds into warm water and turn mousses out onto chilled plates. Coat each with marshmallow cream pulled up into soft peaks. Decorate each with a Pink Chocolate Butterfly.

China molds
To remove a mousse from a china mold, hold it in hand-hot water for the count of 20, to allow the warmth to penetrate.

Champagne Hearts

Six ¼ cup hearts

½ pound rhubarb
⅜ cup sugar
1 Fruit Mousse recipe, but excluding fruit purée

Decoration
2 teaspoons powdered gelatin
Pink or red food coloring
*Frosted Rose Petals**
½ cup light cream

Cook rhubarb with 4 tablespoons water and the sugar. Drain into a measuring cup, pressing out the juice. Reserve. Blend the fruit in an electric blender.

Fold rhubarb purée into the mousse mixture then pour into six ¼ cup heart-shaped molds and leave to set.

Heat ⅝ cup rhubarb juice in a small pan until warm, then sprinkle the gelatin over it and leave for two minutes. Stir over a low heat until dissolved. Add a few drops of food coloring.

Spoon a little of this gelatin over six serving plates and leave to set. Unmold the hearts onto the plates on top of the gelatin and decorate with Frosted Rose Petals. Serve with cream.

Liqueur Barrels

Two ⅝ cup barrels; 6 portions

2 tablespoons powdered sugar
1 unset Fruit Mousse mixture made without fruit
1 tablespoon Tia Maria liqueur
1 tablespoon Grand Marnier
Orange food coloring

Decoration
*¼ cup Toasted Chopped Hazelnuts**
*¼ cup Toasted Chopped Almonds**
3 tablespoons whipped cream

Stir powdered sugar into mousse mixture and divide equally into two bowls. Stir Tia Maria into one bowl and Grand Marnier with a drop of orange food coloring into the other; pour each into a ⅝ cup cylindrical mold or pan. Cool to set.

Dip molds into hand-hot water and unmold mousses on to wetted waxed paper.

Roll the Tia Maria mousse in chopped hazelnuts to coat and the Grand Marnier one in the almonds. Return to the refrigerator to chill well.

Cut into slices and decorate with the cream.

Cream Desserts

Flavor these velvety desserts with delicate fruits, rich chocolate or liqueurs and serve in elegant glasses, or form edible containers from cookies, chocolate or marzipan. This chapter also contains a recipe for zabaglione – a creamy dessert made from egg yolks.

Fruit Fools

Smooth fruit purée blended into whipped cream makes a simple yet delicious dessert. Variations include adding fruit juices, liqueurs and even sponge cake.

Fruit Fool

About 2¼ cups; six portions

1⅛ cups heavy cream
2 tablespoons lemon juice
4 tablespoons powdered sugar
1⅛ cups fruit purée

Place the cream, lemon juice and powdered sugar in a chilled bowl. Beat until it just holds its shape. Gradually beat in the fruit purée and continue beating until the mixture is thick.

   Divide between six small glasses. Decorate and chill for one hour.

   Serve with Brandy Snaps (page 65) or other crisp cookies.

Syllabub

Six ⅜ cup portions

1 egg white
¼ cup Grand Marnier
¼ cup fresh orange juice
½ quantity Fruit Fool recipe, but omitting fruit purée
6 Brandy Snaps (page 65)

Beat egg white until it just holds its shape. Stir Grand Marnier and orange juice together in a pitcher. Gradually beat juice into fool recipe and continue beating until mixture just holds its shape. Fold in egg white. Divide between six small glasses.

   Chill for 30 minutes. Serve with a Brandy Snap.

Previous pages, **clockwise from left** *Chocolate Pots (page 32); Tipsy Peach (right); Athol Brose (opposite); 2½in Crème à la Coeur (page 33).*

Tipsy Peaches

Six filled peach halves

3 firm, fresh peaches (or 6 halves from a can)
3 tablespoons orange juice
1 tablespoon kirsch
3 tablespoons honey
A few drops almond extract
2 tablespoons freshly brewed black coffee
2 tablespoons brandy
½ quantity Fruit Fool recipe, but omitting fruit purée

Decoration
2 slices kiwi fruit

Halve peaches and discard pits (or drain canned peaches). Place orange juice, kirsch, honey and almond extract in a shallow saucepan over a low heat and stir until the honey has dissolved. Increase heat, add peaches and simmer gently for a few minutes, turning them over once, until the syrup has evaporated. Leave peaches to cool, then drain them on paper towels and remove the skins.

   Gradually beat coffee and brandy into fool mixture and continue beating until thick. Place mixture in a piping bag fitted with a large star tube.

   Place peaches, cut side uppermost, on six small serving plates, cutting a little off the bottom of each peach to make it sit firmly. Pipe a large swirl of fool mixture in the center of each peach. Chill for 30 minutes. Cut each kiwi slice in three and place one slice on each portion.

Ingredients, sauces, edible containers, etc that are asterisked in the recipes on these pages are given in detail on pages 147 to 156. For exact page numbers, refer to the index at the end of the book.

Athol Brose

Six ³⁄₈ cup portions

2 tablespoons medium oatmeal
2 tablespoons blanched almonds, finely chopped
2 tablespoons lemon juice
2 tablespoons whiskey
1 tablespoon clear honey
¹⁄₂ quantity Fruit Fool recipe, but omitting fruit
   purée
Rind of 1 small lemon

Decoration
6 strawberries, halved

Toast oatmeal and almonds under a medium-hot broiler until evenly browned.

Stir lemon juice and whiskey into the honey. Place fool mixture in a medium bowl and gradually add honey mixture; continue beating until it is thick. Fold in the nuts, oatmeal and lemon rind.

Place mixture in a piping bag fitted with a large star potato tube and pipe into six swirls in small glasses. Decorate with halved strawberries.

Avocado and Orange Cups

Six ¹⁄₄ cup portions

1 ripe avocado
Grated rind and juice of 1 small orange
¹⁄₂ quantity Fruit Fool recipe, but omitting fruit
   purée
Green food coloring (optional)
6 Chocolate Cases*
4 tablespoons whipped Chantilly Cream (page 122)
2 kumquats, finely sliced
12 Ratafias (page 61)

Halve avocado, discard pit, scoop out flesh and blend in an electric blender with the orange juice and rind until smooth, or press through a strainer. Quickly beat the purée into the basic fool mixture with a little food coloring, if desired. Beat until thick.

Divide the mixture between the Chocolate Cases and chill for 30 minutes.

Decorate with small rosettes of Chantilly Cream and slices of kumquat. Serve with Ratafias.

St. Clement's Creams

Six ¹⁄₂ cup portions

¹⁄₄ cup sponge cake crumbs
1 small orange
1 small lemon
¹⁄₂ quantity Fruit Fool recipe, but omitting fruit
   purée

Decoration
Glazed Orange and Lemon Peel Strands*

Place cake crumbs in six small pots or glasses. Grate rind of fruit. Squeeze juice from orange and lemon and mix them together in a pitcher. Gradually beat juices into the fool mixture in a small bowl and continue beating until the mixture holds its shape. Stir in the grated rinds.

Divide between pots and tap on a hard surface to settle contents. Chill for several hours or overnight to let the juices soak into the sponge. Decorate with Orange and Lemon Peel Strands.

Rhubarb and Ginger Layers

Six ³⁄₈ cup portions

2 cups prepared rhubarb
2 tablespoons syrup from jar of preserved ginger
2 tablespoons sugar
2 pieces preserved ginger
6 small French Meringues (page 120)
¹⁄₂ quantity Fruit Fool recipe, but omitting fruit
   purée
¹⁄₄ cup Toasted Chopped Hazelnuts*
6 Brandy Snaps (page 65)

Place rhubarb, ginger syrup and sugar in a medium pan, cover and cook over a low heat until the rhubarb is soft. Drain and press through a strainer to make a purée. Finely chop the ginger and crumble the meringues. Place a rounded teaspoon rhubarb purée in the base of each glass.

Place half the fool mixture into a piping bag fitted with a large star tube and beat the remaining rhubarb into the remaining fool mixture.

Reserve a little ginger for decoration and fold remainder into rhubarb mixture. Divide half this mixture between the glasses and sprinkle meringues over it with half the nuts. Spoon the remaining rhubarb mixture, then the nuts into the glasses. Pipe a large swirl of Fruit Fool mixture on top of each and sprinkle the remaining ginger over.

Chill 1 hour. Serve with a Brandy Snap.

Custard Creams

This rich, creamy base can be flavored in many ways and set in tiny glasses or edible containers. Cookies, nuts and citrus strands complement its smooth texture.

Custard Cream

About 3½ cups; 12 portions

1 orange
⅛ cup milk
2 egg yolks
¼ cup sugar
2 tablespoons cornstarch
1 egg white, beaten
1⅛ cups heavy cream, whipped

Remove rind from orange with a potato peeler and place in a small pan with the milk. Heat slowly to the boiling point. Leave to cool.

Place yolks, sugar and cornstarch in a small bowl and beat together until pale and creamy. Gradually stir in the strained milk. Return mixture to the pan and beat over a medium heat until mixture thickens and boils. Simmer for 1 minute. Remove from heat and continue beating until the custard is cool. Beat in flavoring, then fold in the egg white and cream. Chill before serving.

Prune Velvets

Six ⅜ cup portions

½ cup pitted prunes
1⅛ cups freshly made tea
1 lemon
½ quantity Custard Cream recipe

To serve
Glazed Lemon Peel Strands*
Toasted Chopped Hazelnuts*
4 Orange and Almond Cigars (page 66)

Place prunes in the tea. Remove lemon rind with a potato peeler, add to prunes and leave to soak several hours or overnight until prunes are swollen and soft. Drain and blend the prunes in an electric blender, using a little juice if necessary, to make ½ cup purée.

Beat custard mixture and gradually beat in prune purée. Divide between four small glasses. Chill. Decorate with lemon strips and nuts. Serve with Orange and Almond Cigars.

Mango Creams

Six ¼ cup portions

¼ cup mango purée
½ quantity Custard Cream recipe
A few drops orange food coloring (optional)
4 tablespoons marzipan
2 tablespoons chopped pecan nuts

To serve
6 pecan nut halves
6 Brandy Snaps (page 65)

Beat mango purée into the Custard Cream, adding a few drops of food coloring if desired.

Grate the marzipan and place in six small serving glasses. Place a little Custard Cream on top and then a layer of chopped nuts. Top with remaining custard. Chill before serving. Decorate each with a pecan nut half and serve with a Brandy Snap.

Pineapple and Walnut Cones

Six 3in cones

¼ cup fresh or canned pineapple
2 tablespoons shelled walnuts
2 tablespoons crystallized ginger
½ quantity Custard Cream recipe

To serve
6 Coupelle Cornets (page 65)
2 small pieces crystallized ginger, sliced
2 glacé cherries, chopped

Drain the pineapple on paper towels and finely chop. Finely chop walnuts and ginger. Fold pineapple, walnuts and ginger into Custard Cream mixture. Divide the mixture between six Coupelle Cornets and serve at once decorated with sliced ginger and chopped cherries.

Right, from top Paska (page 33); 3in Summer Fruit Basket (page 33); Tropical Surprise (page 33).

Chilled Zabaglione

Four ¼ cup portions

2 egg yolks
¼ cup sugar
⅜ cup sweet white wine, Marsala or sherry

To serve
½ cup fraises des bois or raspberries
4 Langues des Chats (page 64)

Fill a saucepan about one-third full of water and place a round-bottomed bowl over the pan to ensure that the water does not touch the bottom of the bowl. Remove bowl and bring pan of water to a boil. Place yolks and sugar in the bowl and, using a small balloon whisk, beat mixture until pale and thick. Set bowl over the prepared pan and pour wine into the eggs and sugar. Reduce heat and do not allow water to rise above a slow simmer.

Using the balloon whisk, beat mixture continually for about 15 minutes until it is thick and has doubled in volume.

Remove bowl from pan and place in a bowl of cold or iced water. Continue whisking occasionally until custard has cooled.

Divide fraises des bois between four small glasses, reserving a few for decoration. Pour zabaglione over fruit and chill for 30 minutes before serving. (To serve warm, whisk over boiling water for about 3 minutes and spoon into tall glasses, omitting fruit.)

Place a Langue de Chat by each portion.

Chocolate Pots

Six ⅜ cup portions

½ quantity Custard Cream recipe
(page 30)
3 ounces semi-sweet chocolate
2 tablespoons dark rum
1 tablespoon freshly brewed strong coffee
⅝ cup heavy cream, whipped

To serve
Chocolate coffee bean candies or Chocolate
Motifs*
12 Langues des Chats (page 64)

Make Custard Cream recipe up to the stage where custard is cooked.

Remove the mixture from the heat. Grate the chocolate and stir into the custard until melted. Beat in rum and coffee and continue beating until the mixture is cool.

Fold in egg white and cream from basic Custard Cream recipe.

Place half the whipped cream in a piping bag fitted with a star tube and put in a cool place to use for decoration.

Fold remaining cream into the chocolate mixture and divide between the serving pots. Tap pots gently on a hard surface in order to settle the contents. Chill.

Pipe a swirl of cream on each pot and add a chocolate decoration.

Serve with the Langues des Chats.

Soft Cheese Creams

This light yet tangy mixture tastes like cheesecake. Replace the full-fat cheese with low-fat soft cheese to reduce calories.

Soft Cheese Creams

Twelve 3 tablespoon portions

12 tablespoons full fat soft cream cheese
2 tablespoons powdered sugar
1 tablespoon lemon juice
Grated rind of ½ lemon
⅝ cup whipping cream, whipped
1 egg white, beaten

Beat cheese until soft. Add powdered sugar, lemon juice and rind, and beat until smooth.

Beat in flavoring as in the recipes on the opposite page.

Beat in cream and egg white.

Pipe or swirl into small containers.

Chill the mixture in the refrigerator for at least 30 minutes before serving.

Tropical Surprises

Six ¼ cup portions

¼ cup raisins
2 tablespoons fresh orange juice
2 tablespoons dark rum
1 firm, ripe banana
½ quantity Soft Cheese Cream recipe
6 Marzipan Flowers*

Decoration
1 teaspoon chopped pistachio nuts

Place raisins, orange juice and rum in a small pan and heat gently but do not boil (or heat in a microwave oven). Leave raisins to cool in the liquid.

Mash banana and beat into the Soft Cheese Cream mixture. Leave to chill for 30 minutes.

Drain raisins and divide them between 6 Marzipan Flowers. Place the banana mixture in a piping bag, fitted with a large plain tube, and pipe mixture into the center of each flower. Decorate with nuts. Serve at once.

Summer Fruit Baskets

Six 3in baskets

½ cup red currants (or raspberries)
2 tablespoons sugar
2 tablespoons water
2 tablespoons Drambuie liqueur
½ quantity Soft Cheese Cream recipe
6 Chocolate Cases*

To serve
6 Chocolate Leaves*

Remove stalks from red currants. Dissolve sugar gently in the water in a small pan or microwave oven. Bring to a boil and cook 1 minute. Remove from heat and stir in Drambuie. Pour syrup over red currants and leave for 1 hour, occasionally stirring. Drain fruit well on paper towels.

Beat 1 tablespoon of the syrup into the Soft Cheese Cream, place in a piping bag fitted with a star tube and pipe the mixture into the Chocolate Cases, leaving a hole in the center. Chill for 30 minutes before serving.

Fill centers with red currants and drizzle a little syrup over. Decorate with Chocolate Leaves. Serve any remaining red currants around the base of the baskets.

Paska

Six 3in portions

2 tablespoons small raisins
1 tablespoon lemon juice
2 teaspoons Amaretto liqueur
2 tablespoons blanched almonds
2 tablespoons glacé cherries (red and green)
2 tablespoons candied fruit peel
2 tablespoons crystallized ginger
2 tablespoons crystallized pineapple
½ quantity Soft Cheese Cream recipe, omitting egg white
6 Coupelle Cornets (page 65)
Frosted Grapes (page 97)

Place raisins, lemon juice and Amaretto in a small bowl and leave to marinate for 1 hour.

Chop almonds into slivers and toast them. Finely chop the cherries, peel, ginger and pineapple, and fold them with the toasted almonds and the raisins into the Soft Cheese Cream mixture. Chill 30 minutes.

Divide the mixture between 6 Coupelle Cornets. Serve with Frosted Grapes.

Crème à la Coeur

Six 2½in servings

½ quantity Soft Cheese Cream recipe, omitting egg white and using cottage cheese instead of cream cheese

To serve
6 Chocolate Shells*
½ cup fraises des bois or raspberries

Line a small strainer with cheesecloth or white paper towels and place over a bowl. Make the Soft Cheese Cream mixture using the cottage cheese instead of cream cheese. Place the mixture in the strain and lightly smooth the surface. Loosely cover with a cloth and leave in a cool place overnight. Turn onto a plate and remove cheesecloth.

Place Chocolate Shells on six small serving plates. Using a soup spoon, scoop out the mixture and place in the center of each shell. Place fruit around the edge of each.

Pies, Tarts

The best pies and tarts have a thin lining of crisp, tasty pastry. Match the type to the filling: crisp unsweetened pie pastry for a sweet meringue-topped pie, for example, and flaky rich puff pastry with a moist filling for covered ones. Top pies with a variety of confections from chocolate curls to a delicious pastry lattice. Open tarts can show the splendor of the filling.

Pie Pastry

This quickly made everyday pastry is the pride of pastrycooks. The fat is rubbed into the flour with cool fingertips or in a food processor. The texture is short and crisp and the type of fat used is important. A mixture of shortening for shortness and butter for flavor makes the best pastry.

Pie Pastry

Four 4in pies, tarts; 6 portions each

1 cup all-purpose flour
2 tablespoons shortening
2 tablespoons butter
Ice water to mix

Place flour in a bowl or food processor and add the fats. Cut the fats in the flour with a knife, then rub in the flour with the fingertips or in the processor until the mixture looks like bread crumbs.

Add about 4 teaspoons ice water and mix to a firm dough. Wrap in plastic wrap and chill until required. To make the following recipes, divide the rubbed-in mixture into four small bowls and flavor three of them as opposite:

Flavorings
Sage
Spread fresh sage leaves on a baking sheet and place in the oven at 275°F, or in a microwave oven, until crisp. Crush the leaves.
   Add 1 teaspoon leaves to the rubbed-in mixture before adding water.

Cheese
Add 2 tablespoons finely grated mature hard cheddar cheese to the rubbed-in mixture before adding water.

Walnut
Add 1 tablespoon finely chopped walnuts to the rubbed-in mixture before adding water.

Quantities
Divide the flavoring ingredients proportionately – by a quarter or a half – to make smaller quantities of flavored Pie Pastry.
   Alternatively, make the full quantities given above and freeze any pastry you do not use.

Previous pages, clockwise from left *Miniature (4in) Pecan Pie (opposite); Quick Lime Meringue Pie (page 41); Blueberry Tarts (page 45); Lemon Curd Tarts (page 48); Coconut Macaroon Tarts (page 49); Chocolate Marron Glacé Tarts (page 49); Chocolate Cheesecake (page 48); Morello Cherry Cheesecake (page 48).*

Cottage Cheese and Currant Lattice Pie

One 4in pie; 6 portions

¹/₄ Pie Pastry recipe, with sage flavor

Filling
1 small egg
¹/₂ cup cottage cheese
1 teaspoon sugar
1 tablespoon currants
¹/₂ teaspoon finely grated lemon rind
Beaten egg to glaze

Prepare a moderate oven at 375°F. Cut off one-third of the pastry and roll the larger piece to line a 4in round 1¼in-deep fluted pie pan. Roll the smaller piece to the size of the top and cut into thin strips.

Mix filling ingredients together and pour into lined pie pan. Cover with a lattice of pastry strips and attach the ends to the sides of the pie with the beaten egg. Brush all over with beaten egg.

Place on a baking sheet and bake 20 to 25 minutes until the filling is set. Serve cold cut into six portions.

Pecan Pie

One 4in pie; 6 portions

¹/₄ Pie Pastry recipe

Filling
2 tablespoons dark corn syrup
2 tablespoons sugar
1 tablespoon melted butter
A few drops vanilla extract
¹/₄ cup pecan halves

To serve
4 tablespoons whipped cream

Prepare a moderate oven at 375°F. Roll out pastry on a floured board and line a 4in round 1¼in-deep fluted pie pan. Press well into the base and the fluted side.

Beat egg and add the syrup, sugar, butter and vanilla. Place the pecans in the pastry crust and pour the syrup mixture over. Place the pie pan on a baking sheet and bake for 30 minutes until the filling is set.

Serve cold cut into six portions with whipped cream.

Chocolate Meringue Pie

One 4in pie; 6 portions

¹/₄ Pie Pastry recipe, with walnut flavor

Filling
2 ounces semi-sweet chocolate
1 tablespoon melted butter
1 egg yolk
1 tablespoon boiling water
1 tablespoon firmly packed dark moist brown sugar
¹/₄ teaspoon ground cinnamon

Topping
1 egg white
2 tablespoons moist brown sugar
A few Chocolate Curls*

Prepare a moderately hot oven at 375°F. Roll out pastry and line a 4in round ¾in-deep fluted pie pan. Roll surplus pastry off the top; chill.

Melt chocolate and butter in a small bowl over a saucepan of hot water or in a microwave oven. Remove from heat. Stir in egg yolk, boiling water, sugar and cinnamon. Pour into pastry crust.

Bake 20 minutes until the pastry is browned and the filling is set. Reduce oven temperature to a cool setting of 275°F.

To make the topping, beat egg white until stiff. Beat in half the sugar and fold in the remainder. Pile or pipe onto the chocolate mixture and dry out for ½ hour. Serve hot or cold cut into six wedges and decorated with Chocolate Curls.

Muesli and Honey Tart

One 4in pie; 6 portions

¹/₄ Pie Pastry recipe, with cheese flavor

Filling
2 tablespoons muesli
1 teaspoon finely grated lemon rind
1 tablespoon lemon juice
5 tablespoons clear honey

Prepare a moderately hot oven at 400°F. Roll out the pastry thinly and line a 4in round 1¼in-deep fluted pie pan. Roll off excess pastry from the top.

Place muesli in the pastry crust. Mix the lemon rind and juice with the honey and pour over.

Place pie pan on a baking sheet and bake in the oven for 20 minutes until the filling is set.

Puff Pastry

Layers of melt-in-the-mouth buttery pastry make a crisp contrast to moist fillings for pies and tarts. Seal the pastry well to prevent the filling boiling out at the high oven temperature that puff pastry needs.

Puff Pastry

18 portions

8 tablespoons butter
1 cup all-purpose flour
1 teaspoon lemon juice
3 tablespoons ice water

Place butter on a plate and mash with a fork until softened. Divide into four portions. Put the flour into a small mixing bowl and rub one portion of the butter into the flour. Mix lemon juice and water and add all at once to the flour. Mix with a fork to a soft dough.

Turn out onto a floured board and knead lightly with the fingertips. Place on a plate, cover with plastic wrap and leave in the refrigerator with the plate of butter to chill for 15 minutes.

Roll out pastry to an oblong 15 × 5in and brush off surplus flour. Take a portion of butter, cut it into small pieces and cover the top two-thirds of the dough to within ¼in of the edges. Fold bottom third up to cover the butter and fold top third over the folded dough. Press the edges with a rolling pin to seal. Turn the dough so that the folds are at the sides and flatten it lightly with the rolling pin. Repeat rolling and folding using another portion of butter cut into small pieces. Cover and chill for at least 20 minutes. Repeat with remaining portion of butter, then repeat the rolling and folding without adding any fat.

Cover pastry and chill for at least ½ hour before using to make the following recipes. The pastry can be wrapped and frozen at this stage, if preferred.

Left, from top *Spiced Apple Crescent (page 40); Omani Almond Pie (above); 7 × 4in Tarte Française (page 40); Spiced Apple Crescent (page 40).*

Omani Almond Pie

Six 2in pies

⅓ Puff Pastry recipe

Filling
2 tablespoons ground almonds
2 tablespoons moist brown sugar
½ teaspoon rose water
Pinch of ground cardamom
Beaten egg to moisten

To serve
6 tablespoons apricot purée

Roll the pastry very thinly and cut out six circles with a 2in plain cutter and the same number with a 2½ in plain cutter.

Mix the almonds, sugar, rose water, cardamom, and 1 teaspoon egg in a small bowl. Spoon the mixture onto the 2in circles, then brush the edges with water. Score the remaining circles with the point of a knife from center to edge in a spiral, then cover each almond mound and seal the edges well. Brush with egg, adding a few drops of water, if necessary.

Prepare a hot oven at 425°F.

Place pies on a baking sheet and bake near the top of the oven for about 10 minutes until risen and golden brown.

Serve with apricot purée.

Marron Glacé Pie

Six 2in pies

⅓ Puff Pastry recipe

Filling
2 marrons glacés, each cut into 3 pieces

To serve
⅝ cup Custard Sauce*

Make as for Omani Almond Pie replacing the almond filling with a piece of marron glacé in each.

Serve with Custard Sauce.

Cherry and Cheese Pie

Six 2in pies

1/3 Puff Pastry recipe (page 39)

Filling
2 maraschino cherries
2 tablespoons cream cheese
1 teaspoon maraschino-flavored syrup from the jar
1 teaspoon beaten egg

Roll out pastry and cut six 2in circles and six 2½in circles.

Chop the cherries finely and mix with the cream cheese, syrup and egg. Place a little filling in the centres of the 2in circles, then finish as for Omani Almond Pie (page 39).

Spiced Apple Crescents

Eight 2in crescents

1 small cooking apple
1 tablespoon sugar
1/2 teaspoon ground cinnamon
1/3 Puff Pastry recipe (page 39)
1 egg white, lightly beaten

Prepare a hot oven at 425°F.

Peel the apple, cut into eight wedges and remove the core. Mix sugar and cinnamon on a plate; coat the apple wedges.

Roll out the pastry thinly and cut out circles about 3in in diameter, ½in bigger than the size of the apple wedges. Brush around the edges with water and place an apple wedge in each center. Fold over the pastry to enclose, and seal each one well. Slash the edges with a knife and flute with the fingers. Brush one side of each crescent with egg white and invert onto the cinnamon sugar. Place on a wetted baking sheet, chill 5 minutes, then bake in the oven until risen and golden brown: about 15 minutes.

Tarte Française

One 7 × 4in tart; 6 portions

1/3 Puff Pastry recipe (page 39)
Beaten egg to glaze
2 tablespoons Apricot Glaze*

Filling
2 tablespoons fraises des bois or wild strawberries
3 green grapes, halved and seeded
10 mandarin orange segments from a can, drained and dried
2 to 3 strawberries, sliced

To serve
6 tablespoons brandy-flavored whipped cream

Roll the pastry and trim to an oblong, 7 × 4in and about ¼in thick. Fold the pastry in half lengthways and cut around the folded pastry ½in away from the edge. Carefully open out each piece. Roll the newly cut-out central oblong and trim to the original size 7 × 4in. Brush the rim of the oblong with water and gently press the border on top, trimming to shape, if necessary. Cut into the edges with a knife. Mark the border in a crisscross design with a knife and prick the inside.

Brush the pastry crust with beaten egg, then place on a baking sheet and chill for about 5 minutes.

Prepare a hot oven at 425°F.

Bake the pastry crust for about 10 minutes until risen and golden brown.

Meanwhile, heat Apricot Glaze gently in a small saucepan or in a microwave oven. Remove pastry from the oven and brush with some of the glaze. Leave until cold.

Arrange fruit in rows in the pastry case and brush with Apricot Glaze. Serve with brandy-flavored whipped cream.

> **Freezing Puff Pastry**
> Cut the Puff Pastry into thirds before freezing for these recipes.
> Alternatively, make up the pies, freeze them on the baking sheets after chilling, then pack in boxes and seal. Cook from frozen, allowing about 4 minutes extra cooking time.

Crumb Crust

This versatile crust can be used baked or unbaked, as a base or topping for pies, cheesecakes and tarts. It freezes well, both cooked and uncooked.

Golden Crumb Crust

Eight 4in pie bases; 32 portions

4 to 6 graham crackers
1 tablespoon light corn syrup
4 tablespoons butter

Crush the graham crackers in a paper bag with a rolling pin, or in a food processor. Melt the syrup and butter in a small saucepan over a low heat.

Chocolate
Add 2 ounces melted semi-sweet chocolate.

Quantities
Divide the flavoring ingredients proportionately – by a quarter or a half – to make smaller quantities of flavored Golden Crumb Crust. Alternately, make the full quantities and freeze any you do not use.

Quick Lime Meringue Pies

Two 4in pies; 8 portions

1/4 Golden Crumb Crust recipe

Filling
1 7-ounce can sweetened condensed milk
Grated rind and juice of 1 lime
1 egg, separated
3 tablespoons sugar
8 pieces candied lime or lime slices

Prepare a moderate oven at 350°F. Press the crumb crust into two 4in loose-bottomed pie pans (or line with foil if the base is solid). Mix milk, lime rind and juice and the egg yolk, and divide between the pans.

Beat egg white until stiff. Beat in one tablespoon of sugar and fold in another tablespoon of sugar. Pile into a piping bag fitted with a star tube and pipe whirls of meringue over the filling. Sprinkle with remaining tablespoon of sugar.

Bake for about 5 minutes until pale golden brown. Decorate with the candied lime or lime slices.

Apricot Pies

Two 4in pies; 8 portions

1/2 cup dried apricots
5/8 cup sweet white vermouth
5/8 cup water
1/2 cup prepared cooking apple
1/2 cup sugar
1/2 Golden Crumb Crust
1/4 cup blanched almonds
4 tablespoons whipped cream

Soak the apricots in the vermouth and water overnight. Place in a medium saucepan and add the apple; cook over a low heat until the fruit is soft and the liquid reduced. Add the sugar and cook, stirring frequently, until the mixture is thick.

Spread two-thirds of the crumb crust mixture into two 4 × 2¼in miniature bread pans. Cover with the apricot mixture then top with the remaining crumbs. Decorate with the almonds. Allow to cool, then chill.

Cut into bars and serve with whipped cream.

Banana Cream Pie

One 4in pie; 4 portions

1/4 Golden Crumb Crust with chocolate flavor
1 small banana
1 teaspoon lemon juice
2 squares chocolate, melted
1/4 cup heavy cream
1 tablespoon Tia Maria
1/2 teaspoon sweetened cocoa powder
2 pistachio nuts, chopped

Line a 4in pie pan with foil and press crumb crust mixture over base and sides.

Slice the banana and coat in lemon juice to prevent browning. Dip half the slices into melted chocolate and leave on foil to set. Spread remaining chocolate over base of pie and cover with remaining banana slices.

Whip cream with Tia Maria and pipe over banana top. Dust with cocoa powder and decorate with the chocolate banana pieces and pistachio nuts.

Pâte Sucrée

This rich sweet dough is the classic French pastry for sweet pies. It is very tender, but easy to handle if kept chilled. Use it for a variety of tarts and pies or flavor and layer it to make delicious tortes. It freezes well both cooked and raw.

Classic Pâte Sucrée

12 to 16 portions

6 tablespoons butter
½ cup sugar
1 egg yolk
1¼ cups all-purpose flour

Cream the butter and sugar together, add egg yolk then flour and mix to a soft dough then knead until smooth. Alternatively, place all the ingredients in a food processor and run the machine until a dough is formed.

Wrap the dough in plastic wrap and chill for at least ½ hour. Use for the following recipes, or freeze at this stage, if desired.

Flavorings

Chocolate
Knead 1 tablespoon cocoa into the pastry with ½ teaspoon milk.

Ginger
Add 2 teaspoons ground ginger.

Hazelnut
Add 2 tablespoons finely chopped Toasted Hazelnuts*.

Quantities
Divide the flavoring ingredients proportionately – by a quarter or a half – to make smaller quantities of flavored Pâte Sucrée.

Alternatively, make the full quantities and freeze any pastry you do not use.

Normandy Flan

One 4in pie; 4 portions

¼ Pâte Sucrée

Filling
1 cup prepared cooking apples
1 teaspoon lemon juice
1 teaspoon sugar
1 pat of butter
¼ teaspoon ground cinnamon
½ teaspoon grated lemon rind
2 teaspoons apricot jam
2 teaspoons Calvados

Glaze
1 tablespoon apricot jam
1 tablespoon Calvados
1 tablespoon sugar

Prepare a moderate oven at 375°F. Roll out the pastry and line a 4in loose-based fluted pie pan; chill.

Cut apples into quarters. Remove the core from one apple, but not the skin, and slice finely. Place on a plate, brush with lemon juice and sprinkle with sugar.

Peel and core the remaining apple and place in a small saucepan with the butter, cinnamon, lemon rind and jam. Stir over a low heat until the butter has melted, then cover and cook slowly until pulpy.

Press through a strainer, cool, add the Calvados and spoon into the pastry crust, spreading it out. Arrange the sugared apple slices, overlapping, on top of the purée and bake for 20 to 25 minutes until the pastry is golden brown.

Meanwhile make the glaze. Place the jam, Calvados and sugar in a small saucepan and stir over a low heat until the mixture is thick and coats the back of the spoon.

Remove the flan from the oven and brush the glaze over the apples.

Right, clockwise from top *Selection of Frangipane Tartlets: Cherry Ripe (page 44); 2in Chocolate Ginger (page 45); Strawberry (page 44); Walnut Coffee (page 45); Peach and Cream (page 44).*

Frangipane Tartlet Bases

Six 2in tartlet bases

½ chocolate-flavored Pâte Sucrée (page 42)

Frangipane
4 tablespoons butter
¼ cup sugar
1 egg
¼ cup ground almonds
1 tablespoon flour
A few drops almond extract
1 tablespoon kirsch

Place various-shaped petits fours molds together on the table. Roll out the pastry and lift over the rolling pin to cover the molds. Roll lightly over the top to cut off the pastry. Press the dough gently into each mold taking care to avoid stretching it. Chill the pastry.

Meanwhile make the frangipane. Cream butter and sugar together, gradually beating in the egg, then the almonds, flour, almond extract and kirsch.

Fit a piping bag with a ¼in plain tube and half fill the tartlet cases with frangipane. If cooking is required at this stage, prepare a moderate oven at 325°F, and bake until the frangipane is set and browned, 20-25 minutes.

Ginger-flavored Tartlet Cases: ½ ginger-flavored Pâte Sucrée (page 42) makes six 2in tartlets.

Hazelnut-flavored Tartlet Cases: ½ hazelnut-flavored Pâte Sucrée (page 42) makes six 2in tartlets.

Strawberry Tartlets

Six 2in tartlets

1 tablespoon Apricot Glaze*
1 teaspoon brandy
6 cooked hazelnut-flavored Frangipane Tartlet Bases (above)
6 strawberries, sliced
4 tablespoons whipped cream
1 teaspoon chopped pistachio nuts

Heat the Apricot Glaze with the brandy gently in a cup in a small saucepan or microwave oven, then generously brush it over the frangipane. Slice and arrange strawberries on top of each tartlet and brush with more glaze. Pipe a swirl of cream on each and decorate with chopped pistachio nuts.

Peach and Cream Tartlets

Six 2in tartlets

2 tablespoons Chantilly Cream (page 122)
1 teaspoon peach purée
Orange food coloring
2 tablespoons Praline Cream (page 122)
6 cooked hazelnut-flavored Frangipane Tartlet Bases (left)
6 fresh peach slices, cut small
Flaked almonds

Fit a nylon piping bag with a small star tube.
Mix, in a small bowl, the Chantilly Cream with peach purée and a drop of orange food coloring. Place the Praline Cream down one side of the piping bag and the peach cream down the other side. Place a peach slice on each tartlet, pipe on the creams and decorate with almonds.

Cherry Ripe Tartlets

Six 2in tartlets

1½ tablespoons Apricot Glaze*
6 cooked chocolate-flavored Frangipane Tartlet Bases (top left)
2 tablespoons heavy cream
1 teaspoon cherry brandy
6 preserved cherries with stems

Heat the Apricot Glaze gently in a small saucepan, then brush it over the Frangipane Tartlets. Leave to cool.

Whip the cream with the cherry brandy and pipe whirls on the tarts. Arrange the cherries on top.

Blueberry Tarts

Twelve 2½in tarts

¼ *Pâte Sucrée (page 42)*
¼ *cup blueberries (or black currants)*
1 teaspoon sugar
1 teaspoon cornstarch
½ *teaspoon grated lemon rind*
2 tablespoons red currant jelly
12 tiny Meringue Stars (page 125)

Prepare a moderate oven at 375°F. Roll out the pastry fairly thickly and cut out twelve 1½in circles. Press into tartlet pans, making the bases thinner.

Mix the blueberries, sugar, cornstarch and lemon rind; divide between the pans. Bake in the center of the oven about 25 minutes until the pastry is golden brown. Cool 5 minutes, then remove from the pans and brush the fruit with red currant jelly. Serve topped with tiny Meringue Stars.

Linzertorte

Six 1¾in tartlets

Pinch of ground cinnamon
2 tablespoons ground almonds
1 teaspoon grated lemon rind
¼ *Pâte Sucrée (page 42)*

Filling
¼ *cup raspberries*
2 tablespoons sugar
1 beaten egg
1½ *tablespoons raspberry jelly to glaze*
4 tablespoons whipped cream for serving

Prepare a moderate oven at 375°F. Knead the cinnamon, almonds and lemon rind into the pastry, then chill. Cook the raspberries and sugar together until pulpy, then cool.

Divide the pastry into six pieces and press four pieces into deep 2in tartlet pans to line the bases and sides. Roll out and cut the remainder into thin strips. Fill each lined tartlet with raspberry mixture and cover with a lattice of strips, first brushing them with beaten egg to secure.

Bake 20 minutes until golden brown, remove from oven and leave to cool five minutes.

Meanwhile gently melt the jelly in a small saucepan or in a microwave oven. Brush tartlets with the jelly. Serve with whipped cream.

Chocolate Ginger Tartlets

Six 2in tartlets

4 small pieces candied ginger
6 uncooked ginger-flavored Frangipane Tartlet
  Cases (far left)
1 Frangipane mixture (far left)
*1 teaspoon Apricot Glaze**
*2 tablespoons Chocolate Fudge Icing**
4 tablespoons whipped cream
1 teaspoon chopped pistachio nuts

Slice three pieces of candied ginger finely and line each tartlet before piping in the frangipane.

Bake as directed, then brush with Apricot Glaze.

Cover with Chocolate Fudge Icing and leave to set. Pipe four shells of cream on each and decorate with remaining ginger and chopped pistachio nuts.

Walnut Coffee Tartlets

Six 2in tartlets

2 tablespoons shelled walnuts
6 uncooked chocolate-flavored Frangipane Tartlet
  Cases (far left)
1 Frangipane mixture (far left)
*2 rounded tablespoons Rich Butter Cream**
2 teaspoons Tia Maria
Chocolate coffee bean candies

Reserve six half walnuts for decoration, and divide the remainder between the tartlets before piping in the frangipane.

Bake as directed then chill.

Flavor the Rich Butter Cream by mixing in the Tia Maria, and pipe it over the frangipane. Decorate with half walnuts or chocolate coffee beans.

Ingredients, sauces, edible containers, etc that are asterisked in the recipes on these pages are given in detail on pages 147 to 156. For exact page numbers, refer to the index at the end of the book.

Cookie Crust

This is a crisp, easily managed pastry that can be rolled very thinly. It is perfect for pies with deep or heavy fillings, makes a good baked cheesecake base and is meltingly crisp for tartlets. Cookie Crust freezes well, both raw and cooked. Prick the base of a pie and brush it with egg white if you fill it before freezing.

Cookie Crust Pastry

36 to 72 portions

1 cup all-purpose flour
2 tablespoons powdered sugar
5 tablespoons butter, softened
2 teaspoons chilled milk

Place half the flour with the sugar, butter and water in a medium bowl and beat together. Add remaining flour and mix to a firm dough.
　Wrap in plastic wrap and chill for ½ hour.

Flavorings

Almond
Add 2 tablespoons ground almonds, 1 extra teaspoon water and a few drops of almond extract.

Orange or Lemon
Add 2 teaspoons finely grated rind.

Cinnamon
Add 1 teaspoon ground cinnamon.

Quantities
Divide the flavoring ingredients proportionately – by a quarter or a half – to make smaller quantities of flavored Cookie Crust Pastry.
　Alternatively, make the full quantities given above and freeze any you do not use.

Smooth Cheesecake Pie

One 6in pie; 18 portions

½ Cookie Crust Pastry recipe

Filling
1 cup medium-fat soft (cottage) cheese
1 teaspoon each of lemon rind and juice
2 tablespoons melted butter
½ teaspoon vanilla extract
1 tablespoon cornstarch
1 tablespoon natural yogurt
1 egg white
2 tablespoons sugar

Prepare a moderate oven at 325°F. Roll out the pastry and line a 6in loose-based round cake pan (or line the pan with foil if it has a solid base). Bake for 10 minutes.
　Beat together the cheese, lemon rind and juice, butter, vanilla, cornstarch and yogurt. Beat egg white until stiff then beat in 2 teaspoons sugar. Beat remaining sugar into cheese mixture then fold in the meringue. Pour over the pastry crust then tap to level the surface.
　Bake in the center of the oven for 15 minutes or until the cheesecake is set 1in in from the sides. (If the cheesecake rises in the center, the oven is too hot.) Leave to cool then chill overnight before serving.

Alternative cheesecake
½ Golden Crumb Crust recipe (page 41) can be used as a base for the cheesecakes, but do not pre-bake.

Right *Selection of 1in Ripe Berry Tartlets: Strawberry, Raspberry, Blackberry.*

Chocolate Cheesecake

One 4 × 4in or 4 × 2¼in cheesecake; 6 portions

⅛ Cookie Crust Pastry (page 46)
⅓ Smooth Cheesecake Pie filling (page 46), omitting
    lemon rind and juice
1 ounce semi-sweet chocolate, melted
1 teaspoon dark rum

Decoration
11 mandarin orange segments
Apricot Glaze*

Set oven at 325°F.
    Roll out pastry and line a 4 × 4in pan or a
miniature bread pan 4 × 2¼in. Bake for 7 to 10
minutes.
    Beat chocolate and rum into the cheesecake
mixture before adding the egg white. Pour into the
pastry crust and bake for 20 minutes. Decorate with
orange segments brushed with Apricot Glaze.

Lemon Curd Tarts

Six 1¾in tarts

¼ orange-flavored Cookie Crust Pastry recipe (page
    46), used to line six 1¾in tart pans

Filling
1 tablespoon butter, melted
1 tablespoon sugar
1 tablespoon beaten egg
2 tablespoons ground almonds
Grated rind and juice of 1 small lemon

Decoration
Slices from a small lemon
1 tablespoon sugar

Prepare a moderately hot oven at 400°F.
    Cream butter and sugar and beat in the egg,
almonds and lemon. Divide between the tarts and
bake until the filling is set, about 10 minutes.
    Place the lemon slices in a small saucepan, cover
with water, bring to a boil and simmer for about 5
minutes until tender. Gently stir in the sugar, then
cook uncovered until the water has nearly
evaporated and the slices are shiny. Cool on
non-stick baking parchment.
    Brush each tart with the lemon syrup and
arrange the lemon slices, cut into wedges, on top.

Morello Cherry Cheesecake

One 6in cheesecake; 18 portions

⅛ Cookie Crust Pastry (page 46)
⅓ Smooth Cheesecake Pie filling (page 46)
1 teaspoon grated orange rind

Topping
½ cup morello cherries
2 tablespoons sugar
1 tablespoon cherry brandy
½ teaspoon arrowroot

Follow the Smooth Cheesecake Pie recipe, but add
the orange rind to the filling. Cook as directed.
    Remove the pits and cook the cherries gently in a
small saucepan with 2 tablespoons water and the
sugar. Add the cherry brandy and arrowroot, stir
and cook until thickened and clear.
    Arrange over the chilled cheesecake and leave
to set.

Sicilian Cheesecake

One 4 × 4in or 4 × 2¼in cheesecake; 6 portions

⅛ Cookie Crust Pastry (page 46)
2 tablespoons candied fruit
1 teaspoon Strega liqueur
⅓ Smooth Cheesecake Pie filling (page 46)
1 ounce semi-sweet chocolate
2 squares white chocolate for decoration

Prepare oven and pastry crust as for Chocolate
Cheesecake.
    Chop the fruit and marinate in Strega overnight
then mix into the cheesecake filling. Chop the dark
chocolate and add half to the cheesecake mixture.
Pour into the pastry crust and bake for 20 minutes.
Cool slowly, then chill.
    Melt the remaining semi-sweet chocolate and the
white chocolate in small separate bowls over hot
water or in a microwave oven. Spread the dark
chocolate over the cheesecake, then swirl the white
chocolate in with it.

To make tartlets

Use chilled Cookie Crust Pastry rolled out thinly. Cut with plain or fluted cutters and line 1in tartlet pans. Alternatively, roll out in a sheet, then wrap pastry around the rolling pin and place over variously shaped tiny metal petits fours and boat-shaped pans. Roll on the top to cut off the pastry, then gently press it into the pans, taking care to avoid stretching it. Chill until ready to use. If baking blind, prick with a fork. If the pastry is to be frozen raw, brush with egg white.

Ripe Berry Tartlets

Eighteen 1in tarts

¹/₄ almond-flavored Cookie Crust Pastry recipe (page 46), used to line 18 petits fours pans

Filling
2 tablespoons softened butter
2 tablespoons sugar
7 tablespoons cream cheese
1 tablespoon Drambuie liqueur
1 tablespoon Grand Marnier
1 tablespoon apricot brandy
3 tablespoons raspberry or red currant jelly
1 tablespoon kirsch
6 blackberries
6 strawberries
6 raspberries
4 tablespoons Chantilly Cream (page 122)

Prepare a moderately hot oven at 400°F.

Prick the pastry with a fork, chill 10 minutes, then bake about 6 minutes until pale golden brown. Cool in the pans, then remove.

Cream the butter and sugar together, beat in the cream cheese, then divide between three small bowls or cups and beat a liqueur into each.

Gently heat the raspberry or red currant jelly in a small saucepan with the kirsch and brush inside each tart. Divide the flavored cream cheese between the pastry crusts, keeping the flavors separate. Place a blackberry with the Drambuie cheese, a strawberry with the Grand Marnier cheese and a raspberry with the apricot brandy cheese. Brush each with the remaining jelly. Serve with Chantilly Cream.

Coconut Macaroon Tarts

Six 1³/₄in tarts

¹/₄ orange-flavored Cookie Crust Pastry recipe (page 46), used to line six 1³/₄in tart pans

Filling
1 tablespoon butter
1 tablespoon sugar
1 tablespoon egg white
2 tablespoons shredded coconut
2 glacé cherries, chopped
1 tablespoon raspberry jam

Prepare a moderately hot oven at 400°F.

Cream together the butter and sugar and beat in the egg white, then fold in the coconut and cherries. Place a little jam in each tart and divide the coconut mixture between the tarts.

Bake in the center of the oven until golden brown – about 15 minutes.

Chocolate Marron Glacé Tarts

Six 2¹/₂in tarts

¹/₄ Cookie Crust Pastry recipe (page 46) flavored with cinnamon, used to line six 2¹/₂in tart pans

Filling
1 ounce chocolate, chopped
2 tablespoons heavy cream
¹/₄ cup unsweetened chestnut purée
1 teaspoon powdered sugar
2 teaspoons brandy

Decoration
1 marron glacé, chopped
6 white Chocolate Leaves, optional*

Prepare a moderately hot oven at 400°F. Prick the tarts with a fork then bake until golden brown, about 15 minutes. Leave to cool then remove from the pans.

To make the filling, heat the chocolate and cream in a small saucepan, or in a bowl in a microwave oven, until smooth; cool. Beat in the chestnut purée, powdered sugar and brandy then place the mixture in a piping bag fitted with a small star tube. Pipe a circle in each tart and top each with a piece of marron glacé. Decorate with a white Chocolate Leaf, optional.

Pastries

Tiny decorative pastries, made from special doughs, can be filled with liqueur-laced creams, custards, fruits and marzipan and topped with icings, caramel or a shower of powdered sugar.

Layered and Shaped Pastries

Several of these recipes use the puff pastry described in Pies, Tarts – combined with other ingredients to create tiny, light-as-air confections. Recipes with filo pastry are also included.

Raspberry Millefeuilles

One 7 × 3in bar; 6 portions

¼ quantity Puff Pastry recipe (page 39)
6 tablespoons raspberry jam
½ quantity kirsch-flavored Diplomat Cream*
⅜ cup raspberries
2 tablespoons powdered sugar

Prepare a hot oven at 425°F.

Roll the pastry and trim to an oblong 7 × 6in. Cut in half to make two 3 × 7in strips and place on a wetted baking sheet. Cook 7 to 10 minutes until risen and browned. Split through the thickness of each and dry out in the oven for 2 minutes; cool, then trim the edges.

Assemble the layers on a serving dish. Spread half the jam and half the Diplomat Cream on the bottom pastry layer. Cover with pastry then spread with raspberries, another layer of pastry, the remaining jam and Diplomat Cream and the final layer of pastry.

Dredge thickly with powdered sugar. Heat a skewer and press into the sugar to caramelize. Repeat, making a diamond design. Cut in six slices to serve.

Baklava

Sixty-four 1in baklavas

Eleven 12 × 10in sheets filo pastry
⅝ cup clarified butter or ghee

Filling
½ cup mixed chopped nuts
¼ cup sugar
1 teaspoon ground cinnamon
1 tablespoon rose water

Syrup
½ cup sugar
Pared rind and juice of 1 lemon
2 tablespoons honey
1 vanilla bean
1 tablespoon rose water

Prepare a moderate oven at 350°F. Keep the pastry covered with a damp cloth. Brush a 12 × 10 × 2in oblong cake pan with butter or ghee. Spread a sheet of pastry over, then brush with butter or ghee. Repeat with three more layers of pastry.

Mix the nuts, sugar and cinnamon and sprinkle one-third over. Cover with another layer of pastry, then butter. Repeat twice more with the remaining filling and two more sheets of pastry.

Add four more sheets of pastry, brushing between each layer with butter. Cut in 1in strips down the length of the pan and across diagonally to form diamond shapes. Sprinkle with rose water. Bake for 35 minutes until golden brown.

Meanwhile, place the syrup ingredients with ⅔ cup water in a small saucepan and simmer 5 minutes. Strain over the hot pastry and leave to cool in the pan.

Previous pages, clockwise from left *Plate of Danish Pastries (all on page 57): Star surrounded by Tivoli with Vanilla Cream filling, Pinwheel, Spandauer, Tivoli with Apple and Raisin filling and 1½in Pinwheel; Almond Cornets (opposite); Baklavas (above right); Fruit Strudel (opposite); Raspberry Millefeuilles (above).*

Almond Cornets

Six 2in cornets

¼ quantity Puff Pastry recipe (page 39)
2 tablespoons sugar
2 ounces semi-sweet chocolate, melted

Filling
2 tablespoons butter
2 tablespoons superfine sugar
1 tablespoon Strega liqueur
2 tablespoons cream cheese
1 teaspoon grated orange rind
2 tablespoons ground almonds
2 drops almond extract
Chocolate Flakes*

Prepare a hot oven at 425°F.

Roll out the pastry and trim to a 12 × 4in oblong. Cut in six long strips. Brush with water then roll around cream horn tins, first placing the point of the tin underneath the end of the strip and rolling the strip on with the wetted side of the pastry outside. Trim the end of the strip then dip the opposite side in sugar. Place sugar-side up on a wetted baking sheet and bake 5 to 7 minutes until golden brown; cool. Spread the inside of each cornet with melted chocolate.

Cream butter and sugar and beat in the liqueur. Divide into two small bowls and add the cream cheese and orange rind to one and the ground almonds and almond extract to the other. Place both mixtures in piping bags and pipe first the almond mixture, then the cheese mixture into the cornets. Decorate with Chocolate Flakes.

Fruit Strudels

Two 6in strudels; 6 portions each

Two large 20 × 12in sheets filo, fila or strudel pastry leaves

Filling
10 tablespoons butter, melted
⅝ cup fresh bread crumbs
¼ cup granulated brown sugar
2 tablespoons blanched shredded almonds
⅜ cup prepared sliced apple
2 tablespoons raisins
½ cup halved apricots, chopped
3 tablespoons powdered sugar
¾ cup sour cream

Prepare a moderate oven at 375°F. Wring out a dish towel in warm water and place on the table. Cut each sheet of pastry in half to make four 10 × 12in sheets. Place one on the dish towel and cover the others with a damp cloth. Mix ¼ cup of the butter with the bread crumbs. Mix half the sugar and almonds with the apple and raisins. Finally, mix the remaining sugar and almonds with the apricots.

Brush the single sheet of pastry with melted butter and cover with one more sheet of pastry and butter. Spread half the crumb mixture over, then the apple filling over half, leaving a 1in border all around. Fold in the border then roll up, using the cloth. Place seam side down on a baking sheet and brush with more butter. Repeat with the apricot filling. Bake for ½ hour until the pastry is golden brown. Sprinkle with powdered sugar, and serve warm or cold with sour cream.

Choux Pastry

"Choux" is French for cabbage and describes the way a ball of this pastry trebles in size when baked and bursts open – like a cabbage.

Choux Pastry

Sixty 2½in éclairs or about 36 profiteroles

5 tablespoons all-purpose flour
⅝ cup water
4 tablespoons butter
2 eggs, beaten

Prepare a moderately hot oven at 400°F. Grease a baking sheet and brush with water. Sift flour onto a plate and place in the oven for 5 minutes then remove and sift on to a sheet of waxed paper.

Place water and butter in a small saucepan and bring slowly to a boil. Remove from the heat, immediately add the flour all at once and beat well until a smooth ball is formed. Leave to cool, beating occasionally.

Beat in the eggs a little at a time then use for any of the following recipes.

Chocolate Orange Éclairs

Fifteen 2½in éclairs

¼ quantity Choux Pastry (page 53)

Filling
2 tablespoons Chantilly Cream (page 122)
1 teaspoon grated orange rind
1 teaspoon orange liqueur

Topping
1 ounce semi-sweet chocolate
½ teaspoon sunflower oil

Fit a nylon piping bag with a ⅜in plain tube and fill with Choux Pastry. Pipe fifteen 2½in lengths onto the baking sheet. Bake for 25 to 30 minutes until risen and golden brown and crisp.

Remove from the oven and slit down one side to allow the steam to escape. Leave to cool.

For the filling, mix the Chantilly Cream, orange rind and liqueur. Pipe cream into éclairs. Break up the chocolate and melt it in a bowl over a saucepan of hot water. Mix in the oil, then dip the tops of the éclairs into the chocolate and leave to set.

Rainbow Profiteroles

Thirty-six ⅜in profiteroles; 6 portions

¼ quantity Choux Pastry (page 53)
¼ cup heavy cream
½ teaspoon rose water
2 ounces white chocolate
Yellow, pink and lilac paste food coloring
¼ cup Bailey's Cream Liqueur

Place the Choux Pastry in a nylon piping bag fitted with a small ⅜in plain piping tube and pipe small balls on a greased baking sheet. Bake for 15 minutes until risen and golden. Cool on a wire rack.

Whip 2 tablespoons of the cream with the rose water and place in a nylon piping bag fitted with a small plain tube. Pierce the side of each pastry ball with a skewer and pipe cream in each.

Melt the chocolate in a cup over a saucepan of boiling water, or in a microwave oven. Dip six balls in the chocolate and leave to set. Add a few specks of yellow coloring to the chocolate and dip six more balls. Repeat with pink and lilac coloring, then more pink and lilac to make a raspberry color. Mix the remaining cream with the liqueur and serve with the profiteroles.

St. Honoré Puffs

Six 2in puffs

¼ quantity Choux Pastry (page 53)
¼ quantity Cookie Crust Pastry (page 46)
1 tablespoon beaten egg
6 tablespoons whipped cream
2 teaspoons Amaretto liqueur
⅜ cup sugar
*6 Chocolate Leaves**

Place the Choux Pastry in a nylon piping bag fitted with a ⅜in star tube.

Roll out the Cookie Crust Pastry and cut six 2in circles. Place on a baking sheet and brush with beaten egg. Pipe a ring of Choux Pastry on each and six stars on the baking sheet. Brush with egg then bake for 12 to 15 minutes until golden brown. Cool then cut the Choux Pastry circles in half horizontally.

Mix the cream and liqueur and put in a piping bag fitted with a star tube. Pipe a ring of cream in each base and reserve remaining cream.

Place the sugar in a small saucepan and heat slowly until the sugar melts and turns golden brown. Dip the tops of the rings and the small stars into the caramel to coat, spearing them on a skewer. Replace the tops then pipe a star of cream in the center of each, if desired. Decorate with Chocolate Leaves.

Praline Rings

Six 2½in rings

¼ quantity Choux Pastry (page 53)
6 tablespoons Praline Cream (page 122)
2 teaspoons powdered sugar

Prepare a hot oven at 400°F. Grease a baking sheet then sprinkle water over.

Place the pastry in a nylon piping bag fitted with a small star tube and pipe 2½in rings on the baking sheet. Bake for 15 minutes until risen and golden brown.

Cool, split and fill with the Praline Cream then thickly sprinkle with powdered sugar.

Right, from top *Selection of Choux Pastries (all on this page): Rainbow Profiteroles; St. Honoré Puff; 2½in Chocolate Orange Éclairs; Praline Ring.*

Danish Pastries

These buttery flaky pastries originated in Copenhagen when Austrian pastry chefs demonstrated their method of folding butter into dough and Danes took the method a stage further and made it into a variety of attractive shapes, adding moist and tasty fillings. It is worthwhile making a large quantity of dough at a time; it is easy to handle and freezes well.

Danish Pastries

Thirty-two 2 × 2in pastries

Yeast Liquid
1 teaspoon sugar
5 tablespoons hand-hot water
2 teaspoons dried yeast

Dough
1 cup all-purpose flour
½ teaspoon salt
2 tablespoons shortening
1 tablespoon sugar
1 egg, beaten
10 tablespoons butter

Egg Glaze
1 egg yolk, beaten
1 teaspoon sugar
1 tablespoon water

Dissolve sugar in the water in a small bowl. Sprinkle on yeast, then leave in a warm place until frothy, about 10 minutes.

Place flour and salt in a bowl. Add shortening, cut into small pieces, and rub in with the fingertips. Add 1 level tablespoon sugar, beaten egg and yeast liquid, and mix with a fork to form a soft dough. Turn out onto a floured board and knead lightly until smooth. Wrap in greased plastic wrap and chill for 10 minutes.

Work the butter on a plate with a round-ended knife until soft (do not melt). Roll out dough to a 10in square. Spread butter in an oblong 9 × 5in in the center of the dough, 2½in from each end. Fold the two unbuttered ends of dough over, so that they just overlap each other in the center. Press edges with a rolling pin, to seal.

Turn dough and roll out to an oblong about 15 × 5in. Fold dough, bringing top third over center portion, then cover with lower third. Lift onto a plate, cover with foil or greased plastic wrap and leave in the refrigerator for at least 10 minutes (in hot weather, leave for ½ hour, or until butter is very firm). Repeat rolling, folding and resting the dough twice more. Chill. Freeze if not required at once.

Shape and fill pastries as described in the following recipes.

For the glaze, beat egg yolk, sugar and a little water together and brush the pastries with the glaze. Place on a baking sheet and leave in a slightly warm place until they are puffy, about ½ hour.

Meanwhile, prepare a hot oven to 425°F. Bake the pastries for 7 to 10 minutes until golden brown.

Fillings

Almond Paste
Mix 2 tablespoons ground almonds with 2 tablespoons sugar, 1 drop of almond extract and 1 teaspoon beaten egg.

Apple and Raisin
Mix 2 teaspoons chopped seedless raisins with 2 tablespoons grated apple, ¼ teaspoon grated orange rind and 2 teaspoons granulated brown sugar.

Cinnamon
Mix 2 tablespoons butter, 2 tablespoons sugar and 1 teaspoon ground cinnamon. Mix in 1 teaspoon each of currants and cut mixed peel.

Vanilla Cream
In a small saucepan mix 1 tablespoon beaten egg with 1 teaspoon flour and 1 teaspoon sugar. Beat in ¼ cup milk, bring to a boil, stirring. Remove from the heat and add 1 teaspoon vanilla extract.

Tivoli Pastries

Eight 2 × 2in pastries

¼ quantity Danish Pastries recipe
1 quantity Apple and Raisin filling
½ quantity Vanilla Cream filling
Egg Glaze (opposite)

Decoration
1 tablespoon thin Glacé Icing*
Flaked almonds

Roll out the dough and trim to an 8 × 4in oblong.
Cut into eight 2in squares.

Spread a little Apple and Raisin filling diagonally
across four squares. Spread the Vanilla Cream filling
over four squares. Fold over two opposite corners
to enclose the filling and overlap in the center.
Brush with the glaze then press lightly to seal. Place
on a baking sheet and leave in a warm place until
they are puffy, about ½ hour.

Prepare a hot oven at 425°F. Bake the pastries for
7 to 10 minutes until golden brown. Drizzle Glacé
Icing over while still hot and scatter flaked almonds
over.

Stars

Eight 2 × 2in stars

¼ quantity Danish Pastries recipe
1 quantity Almond Paste filling
Egg Glaze (opposite)

Decoration
1 tablespoon thin Glacé Icing*
4 glacé cherries, chopped

Roll out the dough and trim to an 8 × 4in oblong.
Cut into eight 2in squares and brush with Egg Glaze.
Roll the filling into eight balls and place one in the
center of each square.

Cut the corner of each square diagonally ⅜in
towards the center. Fold alternate points onto the
Almond Paste, pressing firmly on top to secure.
Place pastries on a baking sheet, brush with the
glaze and leave in a warm place until they are puffy,
about ½ hour.

Meanwhile, prepare a hot oven at 425°F. Bake the
pastries for 7 to 10 minutes until golden brown.
Drizzle Glacé Icing over while still hot and decorate
with glacé cherry pieces.

Spandauers

Eight 1½ × 1½in spandauers

¼ quantity Danish Pastries recipe
Egg Glaze (opposite)
2 canned or fresh apricot halves, chopped
½ quantity of Vanilla Cream filling

Decoration
2 tablespoons Apricot Glaze*
1 tablespoon thin Glacé Icing*
Flaked almonds

Roll out the pastry and trim to a 6 × 3in oblong.

Cut into eight 1½in squares. Brush over with Egg
Glaze.

Divide apricots between the squares. Fold each
point to meet in the center and press gently to seal.
Divide the Vanilla Cream filling between the
pastries, putting a little in the center of each. Place
pastries on a baking sheet and leave in a warm place
to become puffy, about ½ hour.

Meanwhile, prepare a hot oven at 425°F. Bake the
pastries for 7 to 10 minutes until golden brown.

Brush them with Apricot Glaze after baking, then
drizzle Glacé Icing over them and scatter flaked
almonds over.

Pinwheels

Eight 1½ × 1½in pinwheels

¼ quantity Danish Pastries recipe
1 quantity Cinnamon filling
Egg Glaze (opposite)

Decoration
1 tablespoon thin Glacé Icing*
Flaked almonds

Roll out the pastry and trim to a 10 × 4in oblong.
Spread with filling and roll up from the short side.
With a sharp knife cut into eight slices and place cut
side down on a greased baking sheet. Brush the
pastries with the glaze and leave in a warm place
until they are puffy, about ½ hour.

Meanwhile, prepare a hot oven at 425°F. Bake the
pastries for 7 to 10 minutes until golden brown.
Drizzle Glacé Icing over and scatter flaked almonds
over.

Cookies

Crisp lacy cookies can be served with tea or desserts. When shaped into baskets or cornets they can be filled with creams, mousses or ice cream. Buttery cookie mixtures are shaped by piping and swirling, and soft sponge mixtures make delicious drops, pretzels and fingers.

Ground Almond Cookies

Mix, match, flavor and shape these cookies to make an attractive selection. The flavor improves with storage.

Ground Almond Cookies

Eight ¾in rosettes or ten 2in fingers

Rice paper
¼ cup ground almonds
¼ cup powdered sugar
1 egg white

Glaze
1 egg white, beaten

Decoration
8 shelled almonds
3 glacé cherries, chopped
20 shelled hazelnuts
10 angelica pieces

Cover a baking sheet with rice paper. Prepare a piping bag fitted with a star potato tube.

Place ground almonds and powdered sugar in a small bowl and mix together. Add sufficient egg white to make a smooth paste. Place mixture in a piping bag and pipe mixture onto baking sheet, shaping as described below. Leave overnight to dry.

Prepare a hot oven at 450°F. Brush cookies with egg white to glaze.

Bake cookies for 4 to 5 minutes until just beginning to brown at the edges. Remove from the oven and cool on a wire rack. These cookies will keep up to three weeks in an airtight tin.

Rosettes
Pipe rosettes ¾in in diameter. Place a shelled almond and three small pieces of glacé cherry in the center of each one.

Fingers
Pipe 2in fingers. Place a shelled hazelnut at each end and an angelica leaf in the center of each.

Flavors
Lemon
Stir 2 teaspoons lemon rind into the almond mixture. Decorate with small pieces of lemon gumdrops after baking.

Orange
Stir 2 teaspoons orange rind into the almond mixture. Decorate with pieces of orange gumdrops after baking.

Ginger
Decorate with slices of crystallized ginger.

Previous pages, clockwise from left *Brandy Snap Fan and Brandy Snap (page 65); Walnut Ratafias (opposite); Duet Wreath (page 69) surrounded by Nut Tuile (page 65), Cinnamon Flower (page 69), Orange Finger (page 68), Duet (page 69) and Coupelle Cornet (page 65); Orange and Almond Cigar (page 66); plain and chocolate-coated Florentines (page 66); 1in Sponge Drops (page 69) surrounded by Sponge Drop Oysters and Lady Fingers and Pretzels (all page 69), Coffee Kisses (opposite); Ratafias (opposite); Coffee Sponge Drops (page 69).*

Coffee Kisses

Eight ¾in rosettes

*1 quantity Ground Almond Cookies recipe using
sugar instead of powdered sugar*
2 teaspoons instant coffee
Sugar, to coat
*2 tablespoons coffee-flavored Rich
Butter Cream**
*1 tablespoon powdered sugar, to dust
(optional)*

Prepare a moderately hot oven at 350°F. Grease a
baking sheet.

Make mixture as for Ground Almond Cookies,
stirring in instant coffee and making it stiff enough
to handle. Divide mixture into 16 and lightly shape
each portion into a ball. Roll ball in remaining egg
white then in granulated sugar, to coat.

Place balls a little apart on the baking sheet and
lightly flatten. Bake 10 to 15 minutes until set and
crazed. Remove from the baking sheet and cool on a
wire rack.

To serve, sandwich cookies together in pairs.
Dust with powdered sugar, if desired.

Ratafias

Twelve to fourteen 1in ratafias

*1 quantity Ground Almond Cookies recipe using
sugar instead of powdered sugar*
Few drops almond extract
12 to 14 blanched almonds, optional

Prepare a cool oven at 275°F. Grease and flour a
baking sheet. Prepare a piping bag fitted with a ½in
plain tube.

Place sugar, ground almonds and almond extract
in a small saucepan with the egg white, but reserve
1 teaspoon egg white. Beat ingredients thoroughly
together. Place pan over a low heat and cook 3 to 4
minutes until the mixture thickens and comes away
from the base of the pan. Cool slightly then place
mixture in a piping bag and pipe small rounds or
shape small neat heaps on the baking sheet. Top
each with an almond, if desired. Halfway through
cooking, brush over with reserved egg white; bake
15 to 20 minutes until set and lightly colored.
Remove ratafias from the baking sheet and cool on a
wire rack. These cookies will keep up to three
weeks in an airtight tin.

Variation
Use ground walnuts instead of ground almonds,
shape into rough mounds and bake for 20 to 25
minutes.

Lebkuchen

These spicy, honey-flavored cookies are of German origin and their dark gold
color looks good with swirls and stars of icing, or nuts and glazes. The mixture
can be shaped in many ways and will store well, either raw or cooked.

Lebkuchen

Forty 1½in cookies

2 tablespoons soft brown sugar
2 tablespoons butter
8 teaspoons clear honey
1 cup all-purpose flour
½ teaspoon ground cinnamon
Pinch of ground ginger
Pinch of baking soda

Place sugar and butter in a small saucepan and
carefully measure honey into it. Heat gently until
the butter has melted. Remove from heat and cool.

Sift flour, cinnamon, ginger and baking soda
together. Add to the saucepan and beat until
mixture forms a ball.

Knead dough on a lightly floured surface until
smooth; wrap in plastic wrap and leave dough in the
refrigerator for 1 hour.

Heat oven to 375°F. Grease two baking sheets and
prepare decorations as in the following recipes. Roll
out dough to ¼in thickness, cut out shapes and
bake for 8 to 10 minutes until cookies are pale
golden in color. Lift off baking sheet and cool on a
wire rack. Decorate as described below. Store in an
airtight tin.

Lebkuchen Hearts

Ten 1½in cookies

¼ quantity Lebkuchen dough, as recipe
  (page 61)
2 tablespoons pink Quick Fondant Icing*
10 crystallized violets

Cut out and cook 1½in heart-shaped Lebkuchen
and cool on a wire rack. Decorate each heart with
pink icing and place a crystallized violet on each
one.

Pecan Praline

Twenty-five 1in cookies

½ quantity Lebkuchen dough, as recipe
  (page 61)
¼ cup sugar
25 pecan nuts

Cut out and cook 1in round Lebkuchen. Cool on a
wire tray.

Place sugar in a small heavy-based saucepan and
place over a moderate heat until sugar begins to
melt. Add shelled pecan nuts and stir caramel until
nuts are evenly coated with syrup. Using a teaspoon,
place one pecan nut with a little syrup on each
cookie. Work quickly before the caramel becomes
brittle.

The remaining mixture can be turned onto an
oiled baking sheet and crushed to use as
decorations for desserts.

Meringue-Topped Lebkuchen

Forty ¾in cookies

Powdered sugar, as required
½ egg white, beaten
1 quantity Lebkuchen dough, as recipe
  (page 61)
5 glacé cherries, chopped

Stir sufficient powdered sugar into half a beaten egg
white to form a stiff consistency. Cut out the cookies
and place on a baking sheet. Place a small blob of
meringue in the center of each. Bake for 1 or 2
minutes longer than the basic Lebkuchen recipe.
Decorate each with a piece of glacé cherry
immediately. Cool on a wire tray.

Sesame Lebkuchen

Twenty 1½in cookies

½ quantity Lebkuchen dough, as recipe
  (page 61)
3 tablespoons sesame seeds

Sprinkle a lightly floured surface with sesame seeds
and roll out the dough on top. Cut out shapes as
desired, invert onto baking sheet.

Harlequin Aces

Twenty-five ¾in cookies

½ quantity Lebkuchen dough, as recipe
  (page 61)
1 egg yolk
4 shades food coloring

Using small cookie cutters, cut out tiny Lebkuchen
and place them on the baking sheet. Beat 1 egg yolk
with a few drops of water and divide the yolk
between four egg cups. Color each one with food
coloring and brush the yolk over the kuchen. Bake 3
to 4 minutes – do not overcook.

Royal Stars

Ten 1½in cookies

¼ quantity Lebkuchen dough, as recipe
  (page 61)
½ egg yolk
30 pine nuts

Using a star cutter, cut out Lebkuchen and place
them on a baking sheet. Mix half an egg yolk with 3
drops of water and use to glaze the kuchen. Arrange
3 pine nuts on each and bake as recipe.

To hang cookies
Make a small hole in the cookies before
baking, so that the baked cookies can be
threaded with ribbon and hung up.

Right *Selection of Ground Almond Rosettes and
2in Fingers (page 60).*

Langues des Chats

These buttery cookies can be shaped into fingers, circles and curls. They store
well and are useful to serve with ice creams and softly set desserts.

Langues des Chats

Forty 2½in langues des chats

2 tablespoons butter, softened
2 tablespoons sugar
Few drops vanilla extract
½ beaten egg (small)
¼ cup all-purpose flour

Prepare a moderately hot oven at 400°F. Grease two
baking sheets. Prepare a large Piping Bag* from
non-stick baking parchment.

Place butter, sugar and vanilla extract in a bowl
and beat until light and fluffy. Beat in the egg, then
fold in the flour. Place the mixture in the piping bag
and snip off the end to make a ⅜in hole. Pipe
mixture in 2½in lengths onto the prepared baking
sheets, leaving room between each one for
spreading. Bake 3 to 4 minutes until light golden on
the edges.

Remove tray from the oven and quickly and
gently lift cookies with a spatula. Leave to cool on a
rack. When cold, store in an airtight tin.

Coconut and Cheese Snaps

Twenty-four 1½in snaps

1 quantity Langues des Chats recipe, omitting
    vanilla extract and using 4 tablespoons cream
    cheese instead of butter
1 tablespoon shredded coconut
2 tablespoons sugar
2 tablespoons dried coconut slices

Heat oven and prepare baking sheets as for Langues
des Chats recipe. Grease a small rolling pin or thick
wooden handles for shaping. Make up the mixture
using the cheese instead of the butter. Stir in the
shredded coconut and extra sugar.

Using a teaspoon, drop six half spoonfuls of
mixture well apart on the baking sheets. Spread
mixture out to 1¼in. Sprinkle generously with
coconut flakes on each one. Bake 4 to 5 minutes
until the cookies are just beginning to brown round
the edges. Quickly remove from the baking sheets
and leave to set over the rolling pin or handles
When cold, store in an airtight tin.

Sesame Sticks

Forty 2½in sticks

1 quantity Langues des Chats recipe
2 teaspoons sesame seeds

Follow the Langues des Chats recipe, but stir the
sesame seeds into the mixture before filling the
piping bag.

Walnut Viscontes

Twenty 1in cookies
2 glacé cherries
2 tablespoons ground walnuts
½ quantity Langues des Chats batter

Prepare the oven and baking sheets as in the
Langues des Chats recipe.

Finely chop the cherries and mix with the ground
walnuts. Stir into the mixture.

Using a teaspoon, drop six half spoonfuls of
mixture onto a baking sheet and spread each out to
1in. Bake until just beginning to brown on the
edges. Quickly remove from the sheet and cool the
cookies on a wire rack.

Repeat with remaining mixture.

To avoid breaking the cookies
Do not cover the baking sheet with too
many cookies as they quickly become brittle
once removed from the oven.

Coupelles

Perfect for baskets, cornets and tiny rolls, this mixture can be flavored and attractively shaped. Store the cookies between non-stick parchment.

Coupelles

Twenty 1½in cookies and eight 3in baskets or cornets, or eighteen 3in cigars

4 tablespoons butter
2 egg whites
5 tablespoons sugar
½ cup all-purpose flour, sifted
Oil for brushing

Prepare a moderate oven at 375°F. Line two or three baking sheets with non-stick baking parchment. Brush with oil.

Melt butter gently in a small saucepan and remove from heat. Place egg whites in a medium bowl and beat for 1 minute until frothy. Add sugar and beat a further 2 to 3 minutes until thick. Fold in the flour with the butter.

Using a teaspoon drop three half spoonfuls of the mixture well apart on the prepared baking sheets. Spread each to about a 1½in circle with the back of the spoon. Bake 3 to 4 minutes until just turning golden brown at the edges.

Working quickly, remove the cookies with a spatula and shape (see below). Leave to cool on a wire rack. When cold, store in an airtight tin.

Ease each cookie off the tray first, then leave there while shaping the others. This prevents sticking.

Curves
Grease the handle of a large wooden spoon and lay the hot cookies over it until set.

Cornets
Follow recipe for Coupelle Baskets (page 66) but wrap cookies around greased funnel moulds.

Cigars
Wrap cookies tightly around greased wooden spoon handles and hold a few minutes until set.

Nut Tuiles

Fourteen 2½in tuiles or thirty 1in cookies

2 tablespoons hazelnuts, finely chopped
½ uncooked Coupelles mixture, as recipe

Prepare oven and baking sheet as described in Coupelles recipe. Grease a wooden spoon handle for shaping. Stir the nuts into the mixture. Using a teaspoon place 3 spoonfuls – half spoonfuls for smaller cookies – well apart on the baking sheet. Spread batter to about 2½in – or 1in – circle. Bake.

When just beginning to brown at the edges, remove from baking sheet and leave to set over a wooden spoon handle. When cold, store in an airtight tin. Wipe parchment and repeat with remaining batter.

Brandy Snaps

Ten 2½in snaps or fans

½ quantity Coupelles recipe, omitting egg white
2 tablespoons corn syrup
½ teaspoon ground ginger

Prepare oven and line three baking sheets with non-stick baking parchment. Grease three wooden spoon handles.

Melt syrup gently with the butter and sugar in a small pan, or microwave oven. Stir in flour and ginger. Using a teaspoon, place 3 level spoonfuls of mixture well apart on the parchment and spread out. Bake 7 to 10 minutes. When light golden in color, remove from the oven, wait 30 seconds then quickly remove from the tray and roll quickly around the handles. When set, slide off and leave to cool on a wire rack. Wipe parchment and repeat with remaining mixture.

Fans
To shape, fold the cookie quickly into four and lift up the edges to make a frill.

Shaping cookies
Always spread the mixture out on cooled sheets and use a light, circular movement. Never attempt to cook more than 3 cookies at once.

Coupelle Baskets

Eight 3in baskets

½ uncooked Coupelles mixture, as recipe (page 65)
Large pinch ground cinnamon

Prepare oven and baking sheets as in the basic recipe. Grease two or three brioche pans, deep patty pans or small oranges, for shaping.

Follow basic recipe, folding in cinnamon sifted with the flour.

Using a rounded teaspoon, place mounds of batter well apart on baking sheets and spread each out to a 3in circle. Bake. When just beginning to brown at the edges, remove cookies from the sheet and quickly mold each inside a pan or over an orange, shaping with the fingers. Leave for 1 minute to set, then place basket on a cooling rack.

Wipe parchment and repeat with remaining mixture.

Orange and Almond Cigars

Eighteen 3in cigars

1 tablespoon ground almonds
2 teaspoons grated orange rind
½ uncooked Coupelles mixture, as recipe (page 65)
2 ounces dark chocolate
½ teaspoon kirsch

Heat oven and prepare baking sheets as described in the Coupelles recipe. Grease small wooden handles for shaping.

Stir almonds and orange rind into the mixture. Using a teaspoon, drop 3 level spoonfuls of mixture onto a baking sheet and spread each to an oval. Bake 4 to 5 minutes until lightly browned at the edges.

Remove cookies from the sheet and wrap immediately around the prepared handles. Leave to set, then slide them off the handles and cool the cigars on a wire rack. Repeat with remaining mixture.

Melt chocolate and kirsch in a small bowl over hot water and dip one end of each cigar in this mixture to coat. Leave to dry.

Florentines

Twenty 2½in florentines

Use ½ quantity Coupelles recipe (page 65), omitting
egg white and half the flour
2 tablespoons flaked almonds
2 tablespoons glacé cherries
2 tablespoons candied peel
2 tablespoons whipped cream
Rice paper or non-stick baking parchment

To coat
6 ounces dark chocolate

Heat oven to 350°F. Line two baking sheets with rice paper or non-stick baking parchment.

Roughly crush the almonds. Finely chop the cherries and candied peel. Melt butter and sugar together gently in a small saucepan or microwave oven. Stir in the flour, almonds, cherries and peel. Fold in the cream.

Using a teaspoon, place 3 level spoonfuls of batter well apart on prepared sheets. Lightly flatten. Bake 8 to 10 minutes until edges are light golden in color. Remove sheet from oven. Remove rice paper complete with the Florentines and leave to cool on the paper. When cold cut neatly around each one with scissors. If using baking parchment, wait 30 seconds after removing the tray from the oven, then quickly remove the Florentines and leave them to cool on a wire rack. Repeat with the remaining batter.

To coat with chocolate, break up the chocolate and melt in a small bowl over hot water, or in a microwave oven. Using a small scapula, spread the chocolate on the underside of each Florentine and leave to dry, chocolate side uppermost. When dry, store Florentines in an airtight in.

Traditional Florentines
Traditionally the chocolate is patterned with a fork. If serving Florentines without the chocolate coating, cook them on non-stick baking parchment to capture a delicate lacy effect.

Right, clockwise from top left 2½in Brandy Snaps (page 65); Coupelle Baskets (above); Coupelles (page 65); Brandy Snap Fans (page 65).

Piped Cookies

This mixture is excellent for piping delicate cookies. It holds its shape well and may be used with a cookie cutter. A recipe for lady fingers – also piped but made with egg rather than butter – is included in this section.

Piped Cookies

Sixteen 2½in fingers or twenty-four smaller cookies

4 tablespoons butter, softened
4 teaspoons powdered sugar
Few drops vanilla extract
½ cup all-purpose flour

Prepare a moderate oven at 350°F. Grease two baking sheets.

Place butter, sugar and vanilla extract in a bowl and beat until pale and fluffy. Stir in the flour. Place mixture in a piping bag fitted with a small star potato tube and pipe shapes onto the baking sheets, as described in the following recipes. Bake 10 to 15 minutes until just beginning to turn pale golden in colour.

Remove from the baking sheets and cool on a wire rack. When cold, store in an airtight tin.

Freezing
The Piped Cookies mixture may be rolled into two 1in wide sausage shapes and frozen. To use, part thaw then cut into thin slices and bake as instructed. Alternatively, thaw completely and shape or pipe as required.

Orange Fingers

Eight 2½in fingers

2 teaspoons grated orange rind
½ quantity Piped Cookies batter, as recipe

Stir orange rind into the mixture. Pipe 2½in long fingers onto a greased baking sheet. Bake as directed in the Piped Cookies recipe and then cool on a wire rack.

Lemon Oysters

Twenty 1in shells; 10 oysters

Grated rind of half a lemon
½ quantity Piped Cookies batter, as recipe
2 tablespoons Chocolate Fudge Icing*
Powdered sugar to dust

Stir lemon rind into the mixture. Use a large star potato tube and pipe shells about ¾in wide onto a greased baking sheet. Bake, then cool on a wire rack.

Sandwich two shells together at the base with Chocolate Fudge Icing to make an oyster. Dust with powdered sugar.

Ingredients, sauces, edible containers, etc that are asterisked in the recipes on these pages are given in detail on pages 147 to 156. For exact page numbers, refer to the index at the end of the book.

Cinnamon Flowers

Eight 1in flowers

Large pinch ground cinnamon
½ quantity Piped Cookies batter, as recipe
1 glacé cherry
Powdered sugar to dust

Stir cinnamon into the mixture. Pipe stars of mixture about 1in wide on a greased baking sheet. Cut the cherry into eight small pieces and place one in the center of each. Bake as directed in the Piped Cookies recipe, then cool on a wire rack. Dust each lightly with powdered sugar.

Duets

Ten 2½in sticks plus ten 1in wreaths

1 quantity Piped Cookies batter as recipe, but
*   replacing ¼ cup flour with the same weight in*
*   cornstarch*
2 teaspoons cocoa powder
Few drops milk

Heat oven and prepare baking sheets as in the Piped Cookies recipe. Prepare two large Piping Bags* from non-stick baking parchment.

Place half the mixture in one bag. Stir cocoa powder and one or two drops of milk into the remaining mixture to make it the same consistency as the other half. Place chocolate mixture into the second piping bag. Snip off ends to make a ⅜in hole.

Sticks
Pipe two 2½in fingers side by side of one mixture and pipe one finger of the second mixture on top.

Wreaths
Draw 1in circles on a piece of non-stick baking parchment. Lightly grease and place on baking sheet. Pipe eight beads, alternating color, around inner edge of the circles. Ensure that each bead just touches the next one.

Bake cookies 4 to 5 minutes, without coloring the plain mixture. Cool on a wire rack.

Lady Fingers

Twelve 2½in fingers plus ten 1in sponge drops or eight 1½in pretzels

2 tablespoons sugar
1 egg
Few drops vanilla extract
¼ cup flour
Sifted powdered sugar for dusting

Prepare a moderate oven at 375°F. Grease and flour a baking sheet. Prepare two Piping Bags* from non-stick baking parchment.

Put sugar, egg and vanilla extract in a small bowl placed over hot water. Beat until the mixture is thick and leaves a trail on the surface. Sift flour over the surface and carefully fold in.

Divide mixture between the prepared bags and cut off ends to make a ½in hole. Pipe 2½in long fingers on the prepared baking sheet leaving room for spreading. Dust with powdered sugar. Bake 6 to 7 minutes until pale golden. Cool on a wire rack.

Sponge Drops
Pipe the mixture into 1in discs and bake as for Fingers. When cold, these may be served on their own or sandwiched together, or positioned oyster fashion with icing.

Sponge Pretzels
Pipe mixture in pretzel shapes using a ⅜in hole in the piping bag.

Flavors

Coffee
Add 1 teaspoon instant coffee to the Sponge Fingers mixture before whisking.

Chocolate
Replace 2 teaspoons flour with 2 teaspoons cocoa powder and fold into the mixture.

Orange or Lemon
Add 2 teaspoons grated rind to the basic mixture.

Nothing is more tempting than a selection of gâteaux and tiny cakes, with an abundance of cream, nuts, fruit, chocolate and other mouthwatering delicacies. By ringing the changes on a few simple recipes, you can make a variety of cakes to tempt even the most strong willed. Cakes, including most decorated ones, freeze well and thaw quickly, although those with glacé icing can be messy when frozen.

Butter Sponge Cakes

Make well-flavored, firmly textured cakes by first creaming butter and sugar together. Add a variety of flavorings and bake them in different shapes. If you are in a hurry, use the quick-mix method where all the ingredients are beaten together; if you prefer the flavor of butter the traditional creaming method is best. Butter sponge stores well just wrapped in foil, and will also freeze successfully. Make the basic cake the day before if you intend to cut it into shapes – it will be easier to handle.

Butter Sponge

Sixteen 1in cakes in petits fours cases, or one 5in square slab

4 tablespoons butter, softened
1/4 cup sugar
1 medium size egg, beaten
1/2 cup all-purpose flour and 1 teaspoon baking powder
Flavoring (see following recipes)

Prepare a moderate oven at 375°F.
 Grease and line the base of a 5in square baking pan with waxed paper. Grease the paper.

Place the butter and sugar in a small bowl and beat with a wooden spoon, or beat with an electric beater, until the mixture is pale and creamy. Add the egg, a little at a time, beating well between each addition. Fold in the flour with the flavoring, using a metal spoon.
 Place the mixture in the prepared pan, level the top and bake for 20 to 25 minutes until well risen, firm to touch and golden brown. Leave 2 minutes, then turn the cake out onto a cooking tray and remove the paper.
 When the cake is cold, cut and decorate as required.

> **Butter Sponge cake crumbs**
> Make crumbs from any Butter Sponge cake that is left over from gâteaux or other desserts, and store in the freezer. These crumbs are especially useful for uncooked desserts like the ones on pages 80-81.

Previous pages, from left *Rich Chocolate Cherry Gâteau (page 76) and Coffee and Orange Swirl Cake (page 77) on plate; Chestnut and Mango Slice (page 81).*

Honey and Rum Babas

Six ¼ cup babas

4 tablespoons ground almonds
A few drops of almond extract
2 tablespoons milk
1 quantity Butter Sponge mixture,
   uncooked

Syrup
4 tablespoons clear honey
Rind and juice of ½ lemon
2 tablespoons rum
¼ cup Toasted Chopped Almonds*

Decoration
4 tablespoons whipped cream
6 maraschino cherries

Grease and flour six ¼ cup ring molds.

Stir ground almonds, almond extract and milk into cake mixture. Place mixture in a piping bag fitted with a large tube and pipe mixture into the ring molds. Place molds on a baking sheet and bake 10 to 15 minutes until well risen and firm. Leave 1 minute then remove from the molds by tapping firmly on the base over a large plate.

Prepare the syrup while babas are cooking. Place honey, lemon rind and juice and 4 tablespoons water in a small saucepan, bring slowly to a boil, stirring occasionally, then remove from heat and stir in the rum and nuts. Spoon a little hot syrup over each baba while still hot.

Serve warm or cold with a large rosette of cream in the center of each with a cherry on top.

To coat ring molds with flour
Submerge each mold completely in flour, then remove and tap hard on the base to remove excess.

Saffron and Almond Bar

One 5 × 2in bar; 8 portions

½ quantity Butter Sponge mixture, uncooked
A few strands of saffron
A few drops almond extract
A few drops green food coloring
¼ quantity Rich Butter Cream*
12 tablespoons marzipan
2 ounces dark chocolate, melted
Knob of butter

Grease and line the base of one 5 × 3in loaf pan.

Place a piece of foil-covered cardboard down the center.

Divide the cake mixture between two bowls. Moisten the saffron with 2 teaspoons boiling water and leave to infuse. Stir into one portion the almond extract and sufficient green food coloring to make a pale green mixture. Place the almond mixture in one side of the pan and tap to level the mixture.

Strain the saffron liquid into the second bowl, and mix gently until evenly colored. Place the mixture in the other side of the pan and place the pan on a baking sheet. Bake 15 to 20 minutes or until well risen and firm. Leave 5 minutes, then turn out and leave to cool.

Cut each cake in half lengthwise and sandwich back again using half the Rich Butter Cream and alternating the green and yellow pieces. Wrap the cakes in waxed paper or plastic wrap and chill for 20 minutes.

Roll out the marzipan and cut into a 5 × 7in piece. Spread the marzipan with the remaining icing and roll around the cake, seam underneath.

Stand the cake on its end and brush melted chocolate over the marzipan, to coat. Leave to set. Cut the bar into eight slices.

Petits Fours

Sixteen 1in petits fours:
4 Strawberry Cushions, 4 Floral Crowns, 4 Regals,
4 Chocolate Boxes

A few drops vanilla extract
1 quantity Butter Sponge mixture (page 72),
*   uncooked*
2 tablespoons strained strawberry jam
½ quantity Rich Butter Cream*
6 tablespoons warmed strained apricot jam

Stir a few drops of vanilla extract into the sponge mixture. Bake as for the basic recipe. Stir the strawberry jam into the Rich Butter Cream. Split the cake in half through the thickness and sandwich with a thin layer of butter cream.

To make into petit fours, cut the cake into 1in squares or, using a 1in plain cookie cutter, cut out rounds.

Brush warmed apricot jam around the sides and over the top of each petit fours and decorate as preferred (see below).

To Decorate Strawberry Cushions
2 tablespoons Pink Marzipan*
4 rounds of Butter Sponge, coated
*   with jam*
2 tablespoons Toasted Chopped Hazelnuts or
*   Almonds**
1 tablespoon Rich Butter Cream*

Roll out the Pink Marzipan, cut to fit the tops of the cakes and cover cakes. Hold the top and bottom of the cakes and roll in chopped nuts to coat. Decorate each with a tiny piped star of Rich Butter Cream.

To Decorate Floral Crowns
4 tablespoons Green Marzipan
4 rounds of Butter Sponge, coated
*   with jam*
2 tablespoons whipped cream
4 pistachio nuts, chopped

Roll the Green Marzipan thinly and cut into strips the height of the cakes. Roll around the sides of the cakes to cover. Pipe the tops with cream and decorate with pistachio nuts.

To Decorate Regals
1 tablespoon marzipan
4 squares of Butter Sponge, coated
*   with jam*
½ cup Quick Fondant Icing*
A few drops of yellow food coloring
4 crystallized violets or rose petals

Roll the marzipan into balls and place one in the center of each cake. Place the cakes on a rack with a plate underneath. Keep the Quick Fondant Icing warm over a saucepan of hot water then spoon some over two cakes to cover. Tint the remaining icing pale yellow with food coloring and cover two more cakes. Leave to set. Decorate with a crystallized violet or rose petal.

To Decorate Chocolate Boxes
4 squares of Butter Sponge, coated
*   with jam*
Twenty 1in Chocolate Squares*
2 tablespoons Rich Butter Cream* or whipped cream
A few silver dragées or chocolate coffee
*   bean candies*

Cover each side of the cakes with a square of chocolate. Spread the top of each with Rich Butter Cream or whipped cream to raise the height of the cake then place a chocolate square on top. Place the remaining butter cream in a piping bag fitted with a small star tube and pipe tiny stars around the seams and a small swirl on top. Decorate with silver dragées or chocolate coffee bean candies.

Ingredients, sauces, edible containers, etc that are asterisked in the recipes on these pages are given in detail on pages 147 to 156. For exact page numbers, refer to the index at the end of the book.

Right from top *Selection of Petits Fours (this page): Regal with rose petal; Strawberry Cushion; Chocolate Box; Regal with violet; Floral Crown; selection of these on a plate.*

Rich Chocolate Cherry Gâteau

One 5in gâteau; 8 portions

Sponge
1 ounce dark chocolate, melted
½ quantity Butter Sponge mixture (page 72)

Filling
14 ounce can (1¾ cups) morello cherries in syrup
1 teaspoon arrowroot
¼ cup syrup from cherries
1 tablespoon kirsch
1 cup heavy cream, whipped

Decoration
1 ounce dark chocolate, melted
1 ounce white chocolate, melted
    Chocolate Flakes*

Fold melted chocolate into cake mixture and spread in a greased and lined 5 in round cake pan. Bake 20 to 25 minutes until firm to the touch. Leave 2 minutes then turn cake out onto a cooling tray and remove paper. Leave until cold.

Dry the cherries on paper towels. Blend the arrowroot with 2 teaspoons cherry syrup in a small saucepan, add remaining syrup and cook over a low heat, stirring continuously until the syrup coats the back of the spoon. Remove from the heat and leave to cool. Stir in the kirsch.

Draw two 5in semicircles on baking parchment. Divide each semicircle into four wedges drawing in the lines beyond the curve. Spread dark chocolate into one semicircle and repeat with the white chocolate in the other. When set but still soft, cut the chocolate into the portions with a long bladed knife using the extended lines as a guide. Leave the chocolate to set firmly.

Split the chocolate cake into three layers and place one on a flat cake plate. Place one-third of the whipped cream in a piping bag fitted with a large star tube and pipe three circles of cream on the base. Place cherries between the rows, then position the second cake layer on top. Lightly spread the thickened syrup over the cake and leave 5 minutes. Spread half the remaining cream thickly over the cherry syrup and position the final cake layer on top.

Chill the gâteau and remaining cream (including the cream left in the piping bag) for 30 minutes in the refrigerator.

Spread the remaining cream from the bowl thickly around the sides of the gâteau and a thin layer on top. Carefully remove the chocolate wedges from the paper and position the colors alternately on top of the cake. Press Chocolate Flakes around the side of the cake. Using the remaining cream in the piping bag, pipe eight stars of cream around the top edge of the gâteau and position a cherry on each. Chill the gâteau until ready to serve.

To freeze Chocolate Cherry Gâteau
Open-freeze the decorated gâteau, then pack in a box, or fill the gâteau and place in the freezer instead of the refrigerator before the final decorations. Wrap the cake and store up to two weeks. Thaw in the refrigerator.

Glacé Fruit Bombes

Twelve 1in bombes in petits fourrs cases

2 tablespoons cornstarch
½ cup all-purpose flour
½ teaspoon baking powder
Pinch of cinnamon
1 quantity Butter Sponge mixture (page 72),
    omitting the egg
4 glacé cherries, 4 small crystallized pineapple
    pieces, 4 crystallized ginger pieces
Superfine sugar to dust

Stir cornstarch, flour, baking powder and cinnamon into basic mixture and knead until smooth. Place 12 petits fours cases on a baking sheet. Divide mixture into 12, press each into a small circle and use to mold around the pieces of fruit. Place each bombe in a paper case and cut two slits across the top of each. Sprinkle with a little sugar.

Bake in a moderate oven for 8 to 10 minutes until golden. Dust each with a little extra sugar, then leave to cool.

Beaten Torte Sponge Cakes

Firm to cut, this rich beaten sponge cake is ideal for gâteaux and small, rolled or folded cakes. Take care, when folding in the flour or egg whites, that you do not displace the air already in the mixture.

Torte Sponge

One 5in cake

2 eggs, separated
¼ cup sugar
½ cup all-purpose flour and 1 teaspoon baking powder
1 tablespoon oil
4 teaspoons boiling water
Flavoring (see following recipes)

Prepare a moderately hot oven at 350°F.
Grease and line the base of a 5in pan with waxed paper. Grease the paper.

Place egg yolks, sugar, flour, oil and boiling water in a bowl and beat with a wooden spoon until the mixture forms a smooth batter. Beat the egg whites until they just hold their shape and fold into the batter mixture with the flavoring. Spread the mixture into the prepared pan and bake 15 to 20 minutes until firm and golden.

Leave in the pan for 2 minutes, then remove from the pan, remove the paper and leave to cool on a wire rack

Finish cake as in the following recipes.

Coffee and Orange Swirl Cake

One 5½in cake; 8 portions

Cake
½ quantity Torte Sponge mixture
2 teaspoons instant coffee

Icing
Finely grated rind and juice of ½ orange
A few drops orange food coloring
1 quantity Rich Butter Cream*
½ cup powdered sugar
½ teaspoon instant coffee

Decoration
3 tablespoons whipped cream
1 tablespoon Glazed Orange Peel Strands*

Prepare a 7in square baking pan as in the basic recipe. Dissolve the coffee in 1 teaspoon hot water and fold into the basic Torte Sponge mixture. Spread in the prepared pan and bake as directed.

Invert onto a piece of sugared waxed paper. Stir the orange rind, 1 tablespoon orange juice and a few drops food coloring into the Rich Butter Cream.

To assemble the cake, remove paper from the cake and trim the edges. Spread two-thirds of the butter cream thickly over the cake to the edges, then cut the cake into five 1¼in wide strips. Roll up the first strip and place on its end. Continue wrapping strips around to give a spiral effect. Wrap a double thickness of waxed paper tightly around the cake and secure. Chill the cake for 1 hour (or freeze until required).

To finish the cake, place a 1½in deep collar of non-stick baking parchment around the cake and secure. Add a few drops of orange juice to the powdered sugar and mix to a thick coating consistency. Place 1 tablespoon icing in a small bowl with a drop of orange food coloring. Place orange icing in a small waxed paper icing bag. Dissolve the coffee in a few drops of hot water and stir sufficient into the remaining white icing to tint. Quickly spread the coffee icing over the top of the cake, to cover. Snip the end off the piping bag containing the orange icing and pipe zig-zags on the top of the cake. Leave to set.

Remove the paper collar and spread the reserved butter cream around the side of the cake. Smooth, then mark with a serrated icing scraper.

Pipe small stars of whipped cream around the top edge of the cake and decorate with Glazed Orange Peel Strands.

Lime Parcels

Ten 1½in cakes

Rind and juice of 1 lime
½ quantity Torte Sponge mixture (page 77)
4 tablepoons cream cheese
2 tablespoons powdered sugar
2 tablespoons heavy cream, whipped

Decoration
3 tablespoons pistachio nuts, finely chopped
¼ cup powdered sugar
20 long pieces Glazed Lime Peel Strands*

Grease ten 2 tablespoon deep patty pans. Stir 1 teaspoon lime rind into the cake mixture and divide between the patty pans. Bake 10 to 15 minutes until well risen and golden brown. Remove from the pans and leave to cool on a wire rack.

To make the filling, place the cream cheese in a bowl and beat until smooth. Beat in the powdered sugar, remaining lime rind and 1 tablespoon lime juice. Fold in the whipped cream. Split each sponge cake in half and sandwich together with a little filling, spreading the remainder round the sides. Roll each one in pistachio nuts to coat.

Add a few drops of lime juice or water to the powdered sugar to make a stiff icing and cover the tops of the cakes. Decorate the cakes with Glazed Lime Peel Strands.

Summer Fruit Wraps

Six 3in wraps

Cake
Finely grated rind of ½ lemon
½ quantity Torte Sponge mixture (page 77)

Filling
1 tablespoon sugar
⅜ cup fraises des bois or small raspberries

Prepare a hot oven at 425°F. Place a piece of non-stick baking parchment on two baking sheets and draw three 3in circles on each. Brush the parchment with oil. Stir the lemon rind into the cake mixture. Using a tablespoon place 2 well-filled spoonsful of batter on each circle and spread out to the edges of the circles with the back of a small spoon. Bake each sheet separately for 5 to 7 minutes until the discs are set but still pale in color.

Remove the sheet from the oven and immediately loosen the discs with a scapula. Roll them up immediately into tubes pressing two opposite sides together and leave them side by side with the seams underneath until cold.

Sprinkle sugar over strawberries or raspberries and leave to marinate. Divide the fruit between the tubes, spoon a little of the sugar syrup over and serve at once.

Storage
The sponge discs for the Summer Fruit Wraps recipe will soften if stored overnight in a plastic container. Leave at room temperature for a few hours to harden before serving.

Right *Summer Fruit Wraps (this page) with strawberry filling.*

Crunchnut Torten

One 5in cake; 8 portions

Cake
¼ cup Toasted Hazelnuts*, ground
2 teaspoons milk
½ quantity Torte Sponge mixture (page 77)
One 5in Meringue Disc (page 120)

Filling
2 tablespoons brandy
1 cup heavy cream, whipped

Decoration
2 tablespoons glacé cherries,
   chopped
12 tiny Macaroons (page 129)

Fold nuts and milk into the Torte Sponge mixture and place in the prepared pan as for basic recipe. Bake and cool as recipe.

Split the cake through its thickness into two layers and place the bottom layer on a flat cake plate. Beat the brandy into the whipped cream and spread one-third over the cake. Place the Meringue Disc on top and spread another third of the cream over. Position the second piece of cake on top and spread with the remaining cream. Sprinkle chopped cherries over the top, then place the Macaroons around the edge of the cake. Keep in the refrigerator until ready to serve.

Chocolate and Orange Roulade

Whipped heavy cream may be used instead of Rich Butter Cream, if preferred, for this recipe, but the cake should be eaten within a few hours of assembling.

One 6in long cake; 6 portions

½ quantity Torte Sponge recipe (page 77)
2 ounces melted chocolate

Filling
3 tablespoons orange marmalade
2 tablespoons Grand Marnier
½ quantity Rich Butter Cream*
Powdered sugar for dusting

Prepare a 6in square pan as for the Torte Sponge recipe. Make a basic torte recipe stirring in the melted chocolate. Spread in the pan. Bake as for the basic recipe and invert the cake onto a piece of waxed paper dusted with powdered sugar. Remove the paper when cold and spread the cake with marmalade.

Beat the Grand Marnier into the Rich Butter Cream and spread over the marmalade. Using the waxed paper, roll up the cake. Position the seam underneath. Dust with powdered sugar before serving.

Refrigerator Cakes

These can be quickly assembled from larder ingredients. Chocolate is especially versatile and helps to set a cookie crumb mixture. Remember to allow sufficient time to chill and set the cakes before serving.

Truffles

Eight 1in truffles

2 ounces dark chocolate
Knob of butter
1 tablespoon ground almonds
1 tablespoon heavy cream
½ teaspoon orange rind
Pinch of ground nutmeg
2 teaspoons rum
⅜ cup Butter Sponge crumbs
   (page 72)
1 tablespoon coconut flakes, crushed

Place the chocolate and butter in a bowl over hot water until the chocolate has melted. Remove from the heat and stir in the ground almonds, cream, orange rind, nutmeg and rum, and beat together until well mixed.

Sprinkle in sufficient cake crumbs to make a stiff consistency; chill.

Divide the mixture into eight and mold each one in the hands to make a smooth ball. Roll the truffles in coconut flakes and place each one in a petit four case.

Place in the refrigerator for 1 hour to set.

Double Choc Fudge Cups

Twelve 1in cups

Icing
2 ounces dark chocolate
2 tablespoons butter
2 tablespoons beaten egg
2 teaspoons sherry
3/8 cup powdered sugar

Filling
2 tablespoons corn syrup
3 tablespoons butter
2 tablespoons sweetened cocoa powder
2 tablespoons Toasted Chopped
    Hazelnuts*
2 tablespoons multicolored glacé cherries,
    chopped
2 tablespoons seedless raisins
1/4 cup crushed vanilla wafers

To serve
12 Chocolate Cases* made with white chocolate
12 halves glacé cherries

Place dark chocolate and butter in a small bowl over hot water until the chocolate has melted. Beat in the egg and sherry, then remove bowl from heat and gradually beat in the powdered sugar. Leave to cool.

Place corn syrup, butter and sweetened cocoa powder in a saucepan and heat gently until melted. Stir in hazelnuts, chopped cherries, raisins and crushed wafers. Stir in 1 tablespoon chocolate icing.

When cool divide the mixture between the Chocolate Cases, piling it up to a peak. Chill 1/2 hour in the refrigerator.

Leave the icing in a warm place.

To finish the cases, place the icing in a piping bag fitted with a small star tube and pipe icing around each cookie mound, to coat, starting at the bottom. Top each one with a half glacé cherry.

Chestnut and Mango Slice

One 5 × 3in cake; 8 portions

Base
2 tablespoons butter
1/4 cup crushed graham crackers

Filling
1 small mango or sliced mango from a can
16 tablespoons (8 ounces) cream cheese
4 tablespoons sweetened chestnut purée
1/4 cup Butter Sponge crumbs (page 72)
1 tablespoon rum

Decoration
1/4 cup Toasted Flaked Almonds*
2 teaspoons powdered sugar

Cut a strip of non-stick baking parchment 5 × 12in and use to line the long sides and base of a loaf pan with a base measurement of 5 × 3in. Melt the butter gently in a small saucepan, remove from the heat and stir in the graham cracker crumbs. Spread the crumbs evenly into the base of the prepared pan and press lightly. Chill until set, about 1/2 hour.

Peel the mango, remove the pit and slice and chop the fruit. Place the cream cheese in a bowl and beat until smooth. Beat in the chestnut purée and the chopped mango. Spread half the mixture over the crumb base. Sprinkle half the cake crumbs on top and press down firmly. Pour the rum over. Carefully spread the remaining filling on top. Sprinkle the remaining cake crumbs over; press lightly. Bring the ends of the baking parchment over to cover the filling and leave to set in the refrigerator overnight. Lift the gâteau from the pan with the parchment and place on a flat serving plate. Remove the parchment.

To decorate the gâteau, press the almonds firmly around the sides. Sprinkle the top with powdered sugar.

Traditional Desserts

Warming, light pies and tarts, rich fruity Christmas puddings steeped in brandy, sponge cake mixtures and fruit desserts are all included in this chapter. Most of them are especially suitable for winter meals.

Pies and Tarts

Pies and tarts come in all kinds of guises. These traditional versions vary from festive mince pies, originally made with minced beef to give a sweet and savory combination, to sweet syrup and meringue tarts and even a baked jam roll.

Syrup Tart

One 6in tart; 8 portions

½ Cookie Crust Pastry recipe (page 46)
2 tablespoons fresh white bread crumbs
6 tablespoons light corn syrup
Grated rind of ½ lemon
Pat of butter
1 egg, beaten
3 tablespoons cream

Heat oven to 350°F. Oil a 6in cake pan which is 1in deep and use the pastry to line the base and side. Sprinkle the bread crumbs over the base of the pastry.

Place syrup, lemon rind and butter in a small pan and heat gently. Remove from heat and beat in the egg and then 3 tablespoons of cream. Pour over the bread crumbs and place the tart in the oven. Cook for 30 minutes until set and golden brown. Remove from the oven and cool slightly.

Cut into eight wedges. Serve warm or cold with the remainder of the cream.

To remove pastry from shells
Trim the pastry carefully so that it does not overlap the edges of the shells, or it will be difficult to remove.

Mince Pies

Eight 1½in pies

Pastry
½ Cookie Crust Pastry recipe (page 46)

Filling
3 tablespoons thick mincemeat
1 teaspoon lemon juice
Few drops brandy

Glaze
2 tablespoons milk
¼ cup sugar

To serve
3 tablespoons Brandy Butter* or light cream

Heat oven at 375°F. Grease eight 2 tablespoon patty pans, about 1½in diameter by 1in deep.

Roll out the pastry thinly and cut out eight circles, using a 2½in cutter. Line patty pans with the pastry. Re-roll remaining pastry and cut out eight tops using a 1½in cutter.

Place the mincemeat, lemon juice and brandy in a small bowl and mix together. Divide mincemeat between the pie crusts. Brush the pastry tops with water and place moistened side downwards over the mincemeat. Seal the edges. Brush tops with milk and sprinkle with sugar.

Bake pies for 15 minutes until golden brown. Remove from the pans and return to the oven for 1 to 2 minutes if necessary to brown the sides. Sprinkle with extra sugar.

Serve warm with Brandy Butter or cream.

Previous pages, clockwise from left *Lemon Meringue Pie (opposite); 1½in Mince Pie (right); slice of Syrup Tart (above); Christmas Pudding (page 88); Pineapple Upside-Down Pudding (page 89).*

Baked Jam Roll

One 3 × 5½in roll; 8 portions

Butter for greasing
2 tablespoons fresh white bread crumbs
1 cup all-purpose flour
½ teaspoon baking powder
4 tablespoons suet
2 tablespoons light brown sugar
2 tablespoons beaten egg
¼ cup milk
3 rounded tablespoons firmly set blackberry jam

To serve
½–¾ cup light cream, or Custard Sauce* or Vanilla
   Ice Cream (page 136)

Prepare a moderate oven 350°F. Grease thoroughly with butter an 8 ounce bread pan with a base about 3 × 5½in. Coat the ends liberally with some of the bread crumbs. Butter a piece of waxed paper 5½ × 15 in. Position the paper in the pan with the center on the base, to extend over the sides of the pan. Coat paper with bread crumbs.

Place flour, suet and sugar in a bowl and mix well. Add the egg and sufficient milk to make a stiff dough. Knead lightly on a floured surface. Roll dough to an oblong 7 × 10in. Spread jam over dough to within 1in of the edges. Fold sides of the dough over and lightly roll it up. Moisten the end and place the join underneath.

Lift the roll into the prepared pan and sprinkle with the remaining crumbs. Fold paper over to cover and tuck ends loosely down the sides. Bake for 1 hour until crisp and golden brown, uncovering the top after 30 minutes.

Lift the roll out onto a board. Use a serrated knife and cut off ends. Slice remaining roll into eight pieces. Serve at once with cream, Vanilla Ice Cream or Custard Sauce.

Lemon Meringue Pies

Six 3in pies

Pastry
   ½ Shortcrust Pastry recipe (page 36)

Filling
Grated rind and juice of 1 small lemon
2 tablespoons sugar
4 teaspoons cornstarch
1 large egg yolk, beaten
Pat of butter

Meringue
1 large egg white
¼ cup sugar

Heat oven to 375°F. Grease thoroughly the outsides of six 3in canapé shells or ¼ cup patty pans. Roll out the pastry and cut out six circles, using a 3in cutter. Press each circle onto the outer side of a shell trimming where necessary. (Alternatively, line patty pans with pastry, prick and bake blind for 5 minutes near the top of the oven.) Place shells, pastry side uppermost, onto a baking sheet and bake for 10 minutes until the pastry is golden brown and set. Leave a few minutes to cool then carefully ease from the shells. Return shells to the oven for 1-2 minutes to dry off.

To make the filling, place lemon peel, sugar and ⅝ cup water in a small pan over a low heat and stir until sugar has dissolved, then boil for 2 minutes. Remove from the heat. Blend cornstarch with a little lemon juice, then add the remaining juice. Strain syrup through a strainer onto the cornstarch. Return the mixture to the pan and cook for 2 minutes, stirring continuously. Beat in the egg yolk and butter. Cook a further minute, if necessary, until the mixture is thick. Leave to cool.

Turn oven up to 450°F.

To make the meringue, beat the egg white in a clean bowl until fairly stiff. Add half the sugar and continue beating until the meringue holds its shape. Beat in remaining sugar.

Place half the meringue in a small piping bag fitted with an ⅛in star tube. Divide lemon mixture between pastry shells and pipe three rows of meringue "ropes" radiating out from the base of each shell over the lemon mixture, refilling bag with meringue as required. Place in the oven for 2 minutes until the meringue is golden brown, then reduce oven temperature to 300°F and cook for a further 5 minutes to crisp the meringue. Serve either warm or cold.

Fruit Puddings

Old-fashioned fruit puddings are always a delicious end to any meal. Supremely simple summer pudding packs in all the tangy fruits that are at their peak in warm weather and contrasts with the heavier winter offerings in this chapter. Crumble made with apple is truly traditional.

Apple Crumble

Eight ⅜ cup puddings

Butter for greasing

Fruit
¾ lb prepared cooking apples
3 tablespoons sugar
½ teaspoon ground cinnamon
4 teaspoons fresh orange juice

Topping
¾ cup all-purpose flour
½ teaspoon baking powder
4 tablespoons butter
3 tablespoons light brown sugar

To serve
¾ cup light cream, Custard Sauce* or Vanilla Ice Cream (page 136)

Heat oven to 375°F.

Grease eight ⅜ cup pots with butter. Finely chop the apples and place in a medium bowl with the sugar, cinnamon and orange juice. Mix well together then divide the apple between the prepared pots (fruit should fill the pots by two-thirds).

To make the topping, place flour, baking powder and butter into a medium bowl. Cut up the butter, then rub it into the flour until it resembles fine bread crumbs. Stir in the sugar. Divide topping between the pots and lightly press on to the apples.

Bake for 15 minutes until the crumble is golden brown. Serve warm or cold with cream, Custard Sauce or Vanilla Ice Cream.

Ingredients, sauces, edible containers, etc that are asterisked in the recipes on these pages are given in detail on pages 147 to 156. For exact page numbers, refer to the index at the end of the book.

Summer Pudding

Six ½ cup puddings

Butter for greasing
10 thin slices white bread
¾ cup mixed summer fruits: strawberries,
*   black currants, blackberries, raspberries*
¾ cup prepared cooking apple, sliced
¼ cup sugar
3 tablespoons light cream

Grease six ½ cup plastic molds thoroughly with butter. Trim the crusts from the bread, cut each slice into four and use to line the molds, pressing the bread firmly against the base and sides. Cut the remaining bread to cover the molds. Place the prepared mixed fruits, apple, sugar and ⅝ cup water into a medium pan and simmer fruit gently until soft to make about 2¼ cups purée with plenty of liquid.

Divide the fruit and liquid between the molds. Cover the fruit with the remaining bread. Place a piece of buttered waxed paper on top and weigh down with stones or scale weights. Leave overnight in the refrigerator.

To serve, gently run a knife around the edge of each pudding and invert onto a small plate. Serve chilled with light cream.

Right *Baked Jam Roll (page 85); 5½in long, it is served in slices.*

Family Desserts

These recipes include variations on light sponge cakes which are combined with syrup, fruit or other sweet ingredients then baked or steamed, as well as Christmas pudding and a dessert based on rice.

Chocolate Fudge Pudding

One 4½in cake; 6 portions

Butter for greasing
½ cup all-purpose flour
¼ teaspoon baking powder
4 tablespoons soft margarine
1 egg
4 tablespoons sugar
2 tablespoons cocoa powder
2 tablespoons superfine sugar
⅝ cup hot water
3 tablespoons light cream or Custard Sauce*

Heat oven to 350°F. Butter a 4½in diameter charlotte pan or deep-sided cake pan.

Place flour, baking powder, margarine, egg and sugar into a medium bowl. Add 1 tablespoon cocoa powder. Beat ingredients until light and fluffy.

Spread mixture onto the base of the prepared pan. Stir remaining cocoa powder and superfine sugar together in a small bowl and sprinkle over the top of the cake mixture. Pour the hot water over the sugar and cocoa. Bake immediately for 30 minutes until well risen and firm.

Turn pudding out onto a warmed plate and cut into six wedges.

Serve warm with cream or Custard Sauce.

Christmas Puddings

Ten 2in puddings

2 tablespoons fresh white bread crumbs
4 tablespoons all-purpose flour
¼ teaspoon baking powder
4 tablespoons shredded suet or vegetable shortening
6 tablespoons dark brown sugar
½ teaspoon mixed spice
2 tablespoons chopped mixed nuts
⅜ cup raisins
⅜ cup golden raisins
¼ cup dried apricots
¼ cup glacé cherries
¼ cup pitted dates
½ apple
4 teaspoons black molasses
1 small egg, beaten
½ teaspoon brandy
Grated rind and juice of 1 lemon

To serve
3½ tablespoons Brandy Butter*

Place bread crumbs, flour, baking powder, shortening, sugar, spice and nuts in a small bowl and mix together. Finely chop the raisins, golden raisins, apricots, cherries and dates. Stir into bread crumb mixture. Peel and grate the apple, and add to the bowl with black molasses, egg, brandy, lemon rind and sufficient juice to make a stiff consistency. Cover bowl and leave in a cool place for several hours or overnight.

Prepare a large saucepan for steaming. Divide mixture into ten pieces and mold each one into a ball using wetted hands. Tie each pudding in a wetted piece of muslin dusted with flour. Suspend the puddings over a large pan of boiling water by placing two wooden spoons across the top of the pan with the puddings tied onto them. The puddings should hang above the water level. Cover pan with foil, reduce heat and steam the puddings 2½ hours, replacing the water if necessary. Remove from pan and leave to cool. Remove muslin and wrap puddings in clean muslin or waxed paper.

To serve, reheat the puddings by steaming for 20 minutes. Serve hot with Brandy Butter.

Pineapple Upside-Down Pudding

Six 2in puddings

Glaze
4 tablespoons light brown sugar
Walnut-sized piece of butter, melted

Decoration
5 thin slices of pineapple, cored and skinned
1 glacé cherry

Sponge
¼ cup all-purpose flour
⅛ teaspoon baking powder
Pinch of ground cinnamon
2 tablespoons butter, softened
2 tablespoons sugar
2 tablespoons beaten egg

To serve
3 tablespoons cream or Vanilla Ice Cream (page 136)

Heat oven to 350°F. Butter thoroughly six ¼ cup patty pans.

Stir brown sugar into the melted butter and divide mixture between the prepared pans. Cut each pineapple slice into four wedges and arrange three pieces on top of the sugar in each pan. Cut the cherry into 6 pieces and place one piece in the center of the pineapple pattern.

Place flour, baking powder, cinnamon, butter, sugar and egg in a small bowl and beat well until light and creamy. Divide mixture between the pans. Bake for about 15 minutes until well risen, golden brown and firm to the touch. Place a large plate over the pans and invert the puddings onto the plate. Serve warm with cream or Vanilla Ice Cream.

Cups for steaming
As an alternative to saké cups, small individual puddings can be steamed in egg cups or dariole molds; these will only be half full when the pudding is cooked.

Syrup Puddings

Six ⅜ cup puddings

Butter for greasing
6 teaspoons light corn syrup
4 tablespoons all-purpose flour
¼ teaspoon baking powder
2 tablespoons butter, softened
2 tablespoons sugar
2 tablespoons beaten egg

To serve
Maple syrup

Prepare a large steamer. Grease six ⅜ cup saké cups with butter.

Place 1 teaspoon corn syrup into the base of each cup. Place flour, butter, sugar, baking powder and egg into a bowl. Beat ingredients until light and fluffy. Divide mixture between prepared cups. Cover each cup with foil and steam for 10 minutes. Turn puddings out onto a warmed serving plate. Serve hot with maple syrup.

Creamy Rice Brûlée

Six ⅜ cup portions

2 cups milk
3 tablespoons rice
2 tablespoons butter
Grated rind of 1 small orange
½ teaspoon nutmeg
3 tablespoons sugar
1 egg yolk, beaten
3 tablespoons cream

Topping
6 rounded teaspoons light brown sugar

Place the milk with the rice, butter, orange rind and nutmeg in a medium pan and heat until the milk is boiling. Reduce the heat, partly cover the pan with a lid and simmer gently, stirring occasionally, for 30 minutes until the rice is soft and the mixture is creamy. Beat in the sugar and egg yolk. Stir over a low heat, if necessary, until the mixture is thick again. Remove from the heat and stir in the cream.

Prepare a moderate grill.

Divide the rice pudding between six ⅜ cup heat-resistant pots. Sprinkle 1 rounded teaspoon light brown sugar over the top of each, and place under a medium-hot broiler until the sugar melts and bubbles. Remove from heat. The sugar will harden on top. Serve warm.

Fruit Desserts

Fruits must be the world's first convenience foods. Attractively packaged in skins, pods or peels, they combine exotic flavors and textures with delightful colors. Marinate them in juices or fruit-based liqueurs for refreshing fruit salads or combine different kinds of berries in kissels. Firmer fruits can be cooked in compotes or flambéed in caramel syrup.

Fruit Salads

Mix fruits with complementary textures, shapes and colors to make attractive arrangements. Marinate in a syrup with a hint of liqueur, or in fruit juice, and allow the flavors to blend.

Citrus Fruit Salad

4 portions

1 grapefruit
1 large orange
2 tablespoons white rum
2 tablespoons sugar
½ cup heavy cream
¼ cup plain low-fat yogurt
1 teaspoon powdered sugar
1 small lemon
1 lime
2 teaspoons chopped pistachio nuts

Cut the skin off the grapefruit and the orange then cut between the pith to remove the segments. Spread them on a plate and sprinkle with white rum and sugar. Cover and chill until ready to serve.

Beat the cream until thick, then beat in the yogurt and powdered sugar. Cut four thin slices from the center of the lemon and the lime and reserve for decoration. Grate the rinds from the ends and squeeze the juice, then beat into the cream; chill.

Arrange three segments of grapefruit and two of orange in a curve on four small plates and spoon the syrup over. Pipe a swirl of cream in the center of each. Take a slice of lemon and a slice of lime and cut each to the center. Twist and place on the cream mixture. Sprinkle the fruit with pistachio nuts.

Previous pages, clockwise from left *Apricots in Gewürztraminer (page 95); Frosted Fruits (page 97); Kumquat Baskets with Cream Cheese Filling (page 99); Plum with Spiced Nut Filling surrounded by Litchis with Orange Macaroon Filling (page 98); Fondant Dates (page 97); Prunes in Port (page 96); Chocolate-Coated Strawberry and Ground Cherry (page 97); Fondant Ground Cherry (page 97); Red Fruit Kissel (page 100).*

Mediterranean Date Salad

For each portion

1 fresh date
1 piece peeled mango
4 balls cantaloupe
3 slices fresh fig
1 tablespoon lemon juice
1 teaspoon Cointreau

Remove the pit from the date and press the mango in the cavity. Arrange on a serving plate with the melon and fig. Sprinkle with lemon juice mixed with Cointreau.

Melon Salad

4 portions

1 wedge water melon
1 small wedge honeydew melon
1 piece preserved ginger
Juice of 1 lime
1 tablespoon syrup from ginger jar

Remove the seeds from the melons and cut the fruit in balls. Arrange on four plates a ring of water melon with a ring inside of honeydew melon. Chop the preserved ginger and place in the center.

Mix the lime juice and ginger syrup and pour over the melon. Chill until ready to serve.

Irish Strawberry Rings

4 portions

¹⁄₄ cup raspberries plus 4 whole raspberries
2 tablespoons sugar
¹⁄₄ cup heavy cream
¹⁄₄ cup Bailey's cream liqueur
10 strawberries, sliced
4 slices fresh lime

Place 2 ounces raspberries in a small saucepan and heat until the juice runs. Add the sugar and bring to a boil. Strain into a bowl, cool then chill.

Whip the cream until thick, whip in the liqueur and most of the raspberry purée, reserving 2 tablespoons in the bowl.

Place a slice of lime in the center of each plate and arrange the sliced strawberries around. Spoon a little raspberry purée on each ring and place a raspberry in the center of each lime slice. Serve with the cream mixture.

Green Fruit Salad

3 portions

1 lime
6 tablespoons Sugar Syrup*
1 teaspoon Kümmel
¹⁄₂ a ripe avocado
¹⁄₄ of a green-skinned apple
1 kiwi fruit
9 honeydew melon balls
6 grapes, halved
³⁄₈ cup fromage frais

Grate the rind from the ends of the lime. Cut three thin slices from the center and reserve for garnish. Squeeze the juice and add to the syrup with the Kümmel. Peel and slice the avocado and place in the syrup. Slice the apple, cut in wedges, and place in the syrup.

Arrange the fruit on three small plates with slices of avocado on one side, wedges of apple alongside, kiwi slices, melon balls and grapes. Cut each slice of lime to the center, twist and place on the fruit.

Spoon a little fruit syrup over each portion and serve at once with fromage frais.

Tropical Fruit Salad

4 portions

6 tablespoons Sugar Syrup*
1 passion fruit
1 nectarine, cut in 12 slices
1 star fruit, cut in 4 slices
12 wedges fresh pineapple
3 kiwi fruit, cut in 12 slices

Boil the sugar syrup with the scooped-out seeds of the passion fruit for 2 minutes then strain into a bowl. Add the nectarine, star fruit, pineapple and kiwi fruit. Cover and chill for 2 hours.

Arrange on each of four plates three slices nectarine overlapping, one star fruit slice at the end, then three slices pineapple and three slices kiwi fruit. Pour the syrup over and serve chilled.

Orange Fruit Medley

For each portion

6 tablespoons Sugar Syrup*
1 tablespoon lemon juice
3 slices peeled tamarillo
3 slices kumquat
3 slices paw-paw, seeds removed
2 grapes
1 teaspoon white rum

Place Sugar Syrup and lemon juice in a small saucepan and add the slices of tamarillo, kumquat and paw-paw. Bring to a boil, remove from the heat and leave to cool. Arrange the fruit on a plate, with the paw-paw in a curve and the tamarillo and kumquat alternately overlapping. Cut the grapes in slices and arrange in a fan shape.

Boil the syrup to reduce it by half. Add the white rum and trickle over the fruit.

Fruit Compotes

The fruits in a compote can be fresh or dried, and of a single variety or mixed to blend flavors and textures. Include lime or lemon juice or dry white wine to balance the sweetness of the syrup and add a strongly flavored liqueur. Compotes improve if chilled overnight to allow the flavors to blend.

Spiced Apple Compote

6 portions

5/8 cup hard cider
1 cinnamon stick
2 cloves
1 vanilla bean
2 tablespoons Apricot Glaze*
2 ounces light soft brown sugar
Shredded rind of half an orange
1 pound small cooking apples
Juice of half an orange
2 tablespoons Toasted Flaked Almonds*

Boil cider with the cinnamon stick and cloves for 5 minutes. Remove from the heat, add the vanilla bean and leave until cold; strain. The vanilla bean can be dried and re-used. Place the Apricot Glaze, sugar and the spiced stock in a large shallow saucepan and heat to dissolve the sugar. Add the orange rind and cook for 5 minutes.

Peel the apples, cut in quarters and remove the core. Cut into ½in thick slices and spread in the boiling syrup in a single layer. Return to a boil and cook very slowly until tender but still firm. Remove from the heat and add the orange juice. Cover and leave until cold.

Serve in small bowls with a sprinkling of Toasted Flaked Almonds.

Apricots in Gewürztraminer

6 portions

½ cup whole dried apricots
1⅛ cup Gewürztraminer wine
1 strip orange rind
1 tablespoon clear honey
¼ cup green grapes
3/8 cup sour cream, optional

Place the apricots and wine in a glass or stainless-steel saucepan and bring to a boil. Remove from the heat and leave overnight.

The next day, add the orange rind and honey and bring to a boil. Cover and simmer until the apricots are tender, about 10 minutes. Peel the grapes and remove the seeds, keeping them whole. Add to the apricots and leave to cool.

Remove the orange rind. Serve with sour cream if desired.

Pears with Gin and Lime Juice

6 portions

2 limes
2 tablespoons sugar
2 small ripe pears
3 tablespoons dry gin
6 Brandy Snaps (page 65)

Remove the zest of the limes in strips. Place in a saucepan with 6 tablespoons water and simmer until tender, about 10 minutes. Add the juice of the limes and the sugar and stir until dissolved.

Peel, slice and core the pears. Place in the saucepan in a single layer and baste with juice. Cook until just tender, remove from the heat and add the gin. Leave to cool, basting occasionally with the juice.

Serve with Brandy Snaps.

Left, from top *Melon Salad (page 92); Orange Fruit Medley (page 93); Mediterranean Date Salad (page 92); Tropical Fruit Salad (page 93); Irish Strawberry Ring (page 93).*

Damson Compote with Armagnac

4 portions

1⅛ cups red wine
1 stick cinnamon
1 teaspoon grated fresh ginger
1 strip lemon rind
2 tablespoons sugar
½ cup damsons
2 tablespoons Armagnac
⅝ cup heavy cream
2 tablespoons honey

Heat the wine, cinnamon, ginger and lemon rind and sugar, add the damsons and cook very slowly until the skins just break. Remove from the heat, cover and cool. Lift out the damsons with a slotted spoon and place in a serving bowl.

Boil the syrup until reduced by half, add the Armagnac and strain over the damsons. Cool, then chill.

Serve with whipped cream sweetened with honey.

Cherries in Red Wine

4 portions

⅝ cup water
⅝ cup red wine
2 tablespoons sugar
2 tablespoons red currant jelly
Pinch of ground cinnamon
1 cup sour cherries
1 tablespoon cherry brandy
4 small scoops Vanilla Ice Cream (page 136)

Place the water, wine, sugar and jelly in a saucepan. Bring to a boil, add the cinnamon and simmer 5 minutes. Add the cherries and simmer for 10 minutes. Remove from the syrup with a slotted spoon and reduce the syrup by half. Add cherry brandy and re-heat.

Serve hot with ice cream.

Prunes in Port

6 portions

⅝ cup water
1 strip orange rind
2 tablespoons sugar
⅝ cup ruby port
½ cup large pitted prunes
2 tablespoons marzipan
12 blanched almonds
⅜ cup sour cream

Place the water, orange rind and sugar in a saucepan, cover and simmer for 5 minutes. Remove from the heat and add the port and prunes. Leave to soak overnight, then cook gently for 5 minutes. Remove the prunes with a slotted spoon and boil the syrup until reduced by half. Remove the orange rind; shred finely.

Divide the marzipan into 12 pieces and press around the almonds. Press an almond into the center of each prune and return to the syrup; sprinkle with the orange shreds.

Served chilled with sour cream.

Ingredients, sauces, edible containers, etc that are asterisked in the recipes on these pages are given in detail on pages 147 to 156. For exact page numbers, refer to the index at the end of the book.

Dipped Fruits

A selection of bite-size fruits with crisp sweet coatings provides the perfect finish to a meal. Choose firm whole fruits with dry skins such as grapes, cherries, strawberries and ground cherries. Juice will melt the coating. Cut fruits are best coated with chocolate.

Fondant Fruits

To coat ½ cup assorted fruits

½ cup Quick Fondant Icing*, set
4 teaspoons Sugar Syrup*
½ cup black and green grapes (or cherries, strawberries, ground cherries, greengages, peeled litchis or fresh dates)
Food coloring (optional)

Chop the fondant and place with the syrup in a small deep bowl or cup in a saucepan of boiling water. Stir occasionally until the fondant has melted.

Have ready a tray covered with non-stick baking parchment or foil. Hold the fruit by the stalk and dip into the fondant, taking care to make a neat line at the top. Remove from the icing, invert and turn gently until the fondant has set. Place on the lined tray and leave at least 2 hours until set firmly. Repeat with the remaining fruit, tinting the fondant with food coloring, if desired.

Frosted Fruits

To frost ½ cup assorted fruits

½ cup black and green grapes in pairs (or cherries, strawberries, ground cherries, greengages, red currants or peeled litchis)
1 egg white
Superfine sugar

Wash the fruit only if necessary and dry thoroughly on absorbent paper towels. Place the egg white in a small deep container and dip pairs of grapes in to coat all over. Shake off the surplus, then hold the grapes by the stalks over a sheet of waxed paper and sprinkle with sugar. Dip the bases in sugar then leave to dry for several hours in a warm dry place.

Chocolate-Coated Fruits

To coat ½ cup assorted fruits

6 ounces white chocolate
6 ounces semi-sweet chocolate
½ cup assorted fruits (black and green grapes, cherries, strawberries, ground cherries, greengages, peeled litchis, fresh dates, kumquats, orange segments, pineapple chunks or banana slices)
Food coloring (optional)

Grate the white and then the dark chocolate and place in separate small deep bowls or cups. Heat a saucepan of water and remove from the heat. Place the bowls with the white chocolate in the water and leave until the chocolate has melted. Avoid steam or water mixing with the chocolate.

Alternatively, melt in a microwave oven on defrost setting.

Dip the fruit in the chocolate and turn gently to let the excess fall off. Place on a dry plate and leave to set. Repeat with dark chocolate. Some fruits can be first dipped in white chocolate, left to set, then dipped in dark chocolate. If desired, the white chocolate can be tinted with food coloring.

When coating ground cherries with chocolate, push the papery shells towards the stalk, before dipping the fruit in the chocolate.

Filled Fruits

Cut and shape fruits to make containers for exotic mixtures to complement the flavor of the fruit. Citrus fruits with their firm skins make attractive baskets with handles. Softer fruits such as kiwi fruit, peaches, nectarines and bananas are best halved. Sections of orange and pineapple can be arranged around a firm filling to make an attractive basket. Fruits such as apples and pears that become brown when exposed to the air are not suitable for baskets, and peaches need to be used soon after preparing.

Fruits with Soft Centers

Makes 18 filled fruits

2 plums
2 small peaches
2 apricots
2 small nectarines
2 litchis
2 fresh dates
2 grapes
1 small apple
1 small pear
2 kumquats
1 quantity Spiced Nut Filling (above right)
1 quantity Orange Macaroon Filling (below right)
About ⅝ cup orange juice
¼ cup heavy cream

Remove the pits from the plums, peaches, apricots, nectarines, litchis, dates and grapes. Peel and core the apples and pears.

Pile some filling into the centers of halved plums, peaches, apricots, nectarines, apples and pears. Press filling into the centers of the litchis, dates, grapes and kumquats and re-form the fruit.

Prepare a moderate oven at 375°F. Place the fruit in a shallow ovenproof dish and pour orange juice into the dish to cover the base. Bake in the center of the oven until the fruit is just tender, 15 to 20 minutes. Test by piercing with a toothpick.

Arrange the fruit on small plates and spoon a little juice around. Pour a little cream into the juice and swirl gently with a teaspoon. Serve hot or cold.

Spiced Nut Filling

To fill 9 assorted fruits

2 tablespoons ground almonds
2 tablespoons Toasted Hazelnuts*, finely chopped
2 tablespoons walnuts, finely chopped
2 tablespoons crystallized ginger, chopped
3 tablespoons mincemeat
2 tablespoons dark rum
½ teaspoon ground cinnamon
Finely grated rind of 1 lemon
1 egg yolk

Mix all the ingredients together and use to fill prepared fruits. Bake as directed under Fruits with Soft Centers.

Orange Macaroon Filling

To fill 9 assorted fruits

2 tablespoons butter
2 tablespoons powdered sugar
1 egg yolk
1 teaspoon grated orange rind
1 tablespoon Grand Marnier liqueur
1 tablespoon orange juice
⅜ cup macaroons, crushed

Cream the butter and sugar until light and fluffy. Beat in the egg yolk and orange rind, then the liqueur and orange juice a little at a time. Fold in the macaroons and leave for 5 minutes for the flavors to blend.

Use to fill the prepared fruits and bake as directed under Fruits with Soft Centers.

Citrus Fruit Basket

1 citrus fruit
1 quantity Marzipan or Cream Cheese Filling
  (opposite)

Use a felt pen to draw around the skin of a citrus fruit (kumquat, small orange, lime or lemon) half way from top to bottom, but leaving a ½in "handle" across the top. With a sharp knife cut out the marked section a little away from the line to remove the section and the marking. Cut a small section off the base of the basket if it does not stand evenly on the plate. Gently cut out and scoop out the fruit, taking care to avoid damaging the handle. Press the removed fruit through a strainer and add the purée or juice to the filling ingredients. Pile the filling back into the basket.

Half Fruit Baskets

Use for kiwi fruit, bananas, tamarillos, apricots, peaches and nectarines. Cut the fruit in half, remove pits or seeds as appropriate, and cut a little fruit off each end if necessary for the halves to sit firmly on the plate. Carefully cut around the edges, leaving a thin "wall" to hold the fruit firmly.

Press the removed fruit through a nylon strainer and mix with Marzipan or Cream Cheese Filling.

Marzipan Filling

Fills about ½ cup fruit

2 tablespoons ground almonds
2 tablespoons powdered sugar
1 teaspoon egg white
2 teaspoons brandy
A few drops almond extract
Cake crumbs

Mix the ingredients, together with the purée or juice from the fruit baskets, and add sufficient cake crumbs to make the mixture firm enough to handle.

Cream Cheese Filling

Fills about ½ cup fruit

2 tablespoons butter
2 tablespoons powdered sugar
¼ cup cream cheese, softened
1 tablespoon cognac
Cake crumbs

Cream butter and sugar together until soft and fluffy. Beat in the cream cheese, cognac and fruit juice or purée from the baskets. Add sufficient cake crumbs to make the mixture firm enough to handle.

Kissels

These mixtures of softly set fruits are called Kissels in Eastern Europe, Red Fruit Pudding in Scandinavia and Red Grits in northern Germany. Serve these clear, bright desserts in elegant glasses and top with soft cream if desired.

Rhubarb and Orange Kissel

6 portions in ½ cup glasses

1 cup rhubarb cut in ½in pieces
½ cup sugar
2 tablespoons water
1 orange
2 teaspoons arrowroot
2 tablespoons dry sherry
1 teaspoon superfine sugar
¼ cup lightly whipped cream

In a medium pan, dissolve the sugar in the water. Pare two strips of orange and add to the syrup.

Bring to a boil and add the rhubarb; return to a boil, turn off the heat, cover and leave for 10 minutes.

Cut another strip of orange rind and shred finely; reserve for decoration. Use a serrated knife to cut the remaining peel and pith off the orange. Cut out the segments and add to the pan. Blend the arrowroot with the sherry and add to the fruit. Bring to a boil, stirring. Add more sugar, if desired.

Cool the rhubarb and orange mixture and pour into four glasses. Sprinkle superfine sugar over each portion, then chill.

Pour on the cream and decorate with reserved orange shreds.

Red Fruit Kissel

4 portions in ½ cup glasses

¼ cup black currants
¼ cup red currants
⅝ cup water
¼ cup muscovado light brown sugar
1 cinnamon stick
¼ cup loganberries
¼ cup wild strawberries
2 teaspoons arrowroot
1 tablespoon cherry brandy
1 teaspoon sugar

Remove the stalks from the black currants and red currants and place in a small saucepan with the water, sugar and cinnamon. Bring to a boil, cover and cook 2 minutes. Add the loganberries and strawberries and bring to a boil; remove the cinnamon stick. Blend the arrowroot with the cherry brandy, add to the fruit and bring to a boil, stirring. Stir gently until cooked, then pour into four small glasses. Sprinkle the surface with sugar and leave to cool. Serve chilled.

Golden Fruit Kissel

6 portions in ½ cup glasses

4 golden plums
4 apricots
4 kumquats, sliced
⅝ cup sweet white wine
¼ cup peeled mango
2 teaspoons arrowroot
¼ cup granulated light brown sugar
2 tablespoons Amaretto liqueur
1 teaspoon sugar
¼ cup sour cream

Cut the plums and apricots in halves and remove the pits. Chop the fruit, then place in a small saucepan with the kumquats and wine, bring to a boil, cover and simmer 5 minutes. Remove 6 kumquat slices and reserve for decoration. Cut the mango into small cubes and add.

Blend the arrowroot with the sugar and liqueur. Add to the fruit mixture, bring to a boil, stirring. Remove from heat and cool. Pour into six small glasses, sprinkle with caster sugar and leave to cool.

To serve, beat sour cream and pour over the surface. Decorate each with a kumquat slice.

Spiced Blackberry and Apple Kissel

6 portions in ½ cup glasses

¾ cup apple juice
1 vanilla bean
1 cinnamon stick
2 cloves
1½ in piece fresh ginger, grated
1 cooking apple, peeled, cored and chopped
½ cup blackberries
¼ cup muscovado light brown sugar
2 teaspoons arrowroot or cornstarch
2 tablespoons cognac
1 teaspoon superfine sugar
¼ cup heavy cream
6 slices apple
1 teaspoon lemon juice

Place the apple juice in a small saucepan and add the vanilla bean, cinnamon stick, cloves and ginger. Bring to a boil, cover and leave to infuse 10 minutes. Strain and return the juice to the saucepan. Add the apple, blackberries and brown sugar. Bring to a boil, cover and cook about 2 minutes, until the fruit is tender but whole.

Blend the arrowroot or cornstarch with the brandy and add to the fruit. Bring to a boil, stirring gently. Cool slightly then pour into six glasses. Sprinkle sugar over the surface. Cool, then chill.

To serve, whip the cream until it just holds its shape and pour over the fruit. Decorate each glass with a slice of apple, first brushed with lemon juice to prevent browning.

Flambéed Fruits

Before starting to flambé, collect all the ingredients, cut them into small bite-size pieces and arrange them attractively on a tray. The fruits are then fried, and turned in a light caramel sauce; liqueur is added and flamed to concentrate the flavor and release the alcohol. Serve immediately. Firm fruits such as pineapple, banana, peaches, nectarines, apricots, cherries and pears are best.
Use a spirit or fondue bourguignonne heater, and an attractive copper frying pan; and remember that the pieces of fruit must be at room temperature for successful flambéing.

Flambéed Fruit

4 portions

About ¾ cup prepared fruit
2 tablespoons butter
¼ cup sugar
1 teaspoon orange rind
Juice of 1 small orange and 1 lemon
1 tablespoon liqueur
2 teaspoons liquor

Quickly fry the fruit in half the melted butter; remove from the pan and keep warm. Add the remaining butter and sugar to the pan and stir over a low heat until the sugar has turned golden brown. Add the orange and lemon juices and the rind and stir to dissolve the caramel. Cook over high heat for about 1 minute until the sauce thickens.

   Return the fruit to the pan and heat. Pour over the liqueur and liquor, ignite and leave the flames to die down before spooning some fruit and sauce onto serving plates.

> Ingredients, sauces, edible containers, etc that are asterisked in the recipes on these pages are given in detail on pages 147 to 156. For exact page numbers, refer to the index at the end of the book.

Fruits

Pineapple
Cut one ring for each portion from a fresh pineapple. Use Cointreau and dark rum.

Banana
Half a banana is sufficient for each portion; cut in diagonal slices. Use Malibu and white rum.

Peaches
Use fresh peaches, if possible, and allow half per portion. Cut the fruit in slices and use Grand Marnier and brandy.

Nectarines
Serve half per portion, cut in slices. Use Benedictine and brandy.

Apricots
Serve one apricot per portion, cut in half. Use Amaretto and brandy.

Cherries
Use morello cherries and replace the orange juice with 4 tablespoons red wine and add 1 tablespoon red currant jelly. Use kirsch and brandy.

Pears
Serve half a ripe pear for each portion; peel and cut in thick slices. Use Galliano and vodka.

Batters, Deep-Fried Desserts

Doughnuts, crêpes, fritters, waffles and delicious confections made from potato pastry and even bread are included in this chapter. Fry them quickly, at the correct temperature, to make sure they absorb as little oil as possible. All can be served with a variety of fillings and accompaniments.

Doughnuts

Traditional doughnuts are made with a rich yeast mixture, but these are deliciously "short" textured. The basic recipe can be adapted to make delicious honey cakes.

Doughnuts

Ten 2in doughnuts

3/8 cup all-purpose flour sifted together with 1/2 teaspoon baking powder
2 tablespoons sugar
2 tablespoons margarine
2 tablespoons beaten egg
1 tablespoon milk
Superfine sugar

Prepare a deep-fat fryer and heat oil to 370°F.

Place flour and sugar in a medium bowl. Add margarine, cut up, and rub in until it resembles fine bread crumbs. Add egg and sufficient milk to make a smooth dough. Knead lightly on a floured surface. Roll out to 1/4in thickness. Using a 2in cutter, cut out the doughnuts, then use a 1 1/4in cookie cutter to remove the centers.

Fry doughnuts about 2 minutes or until golden brown on both sides. Drain on paper towels and coat with superfine sugar. Serve warm or cold.

Almond and Honey Balls

Ten 2in balls

2 tablespoons ground almonds
1/2 teaspoon almond extract
1 quantity Doughnut recipe, uncooked

Syrup
6 tablespoons clear honey
1 tablespoon lemon juice
1 tablespoon dark rum
1 tablespoon Toasted Chopped Almonds*

To serve
6 tablespoons Greek yogurt
10 small pieces of honeycomb

Mix the ground almonds and extract into the dough and use extra milk, if necessary to make a soft dough. Drop teaspoonfuls of the mixture onto a lightly floured surface and gently roll to make neat balls. Fry in a deep-fat fryer for 3 to 4 minutes until deep golden brown. Drain on paper towels. Place balls in a small bowl.

To make the syrup, gently warm the honey, lemon juice and rum. Stir in the nuts. Pour syrup over balls and turn them over several times to coat. They can be served warm or cold.

To serve, spread a tablespoon (15ml spoon) of yogurt on a plate and place an Almond and Honey Ball on top. Decorate the plate with a piece of honeycomb.

Previous pages, clockwise from left *Maple and Vanilla Waffle (page 108); Mincemeat Curls (page 109); Peaches and Praline Cream crêpe (page 112); 2in Almond and Honey Ball (right); Doughnuts (above).*

Perfect frying
Do not allow the fat to get too hot the outside will become overcooked before the inside is set.

Chocolate Surprises

Four 2in filled doughnuts

½ quantity Doughnut recipe, uncooked
4 pieces thin semi-sweet chocolate
Powdered sugar, to coat
1 teaspoon kirsch
About 16 canned orange segments

Roll out the dough to ⅛in thickness and cut out four circles using a 3in cutter. Place a piece of chocolate in the center of each. Brush the outside edge of each circle with water and draw up to enclose the chocolate; seal well. Turn the doughnut over with the join underneath and gently flatten with a rolling pin to a 2in round (or smaller if the chocolate begins to show through).

Fry doughnuts in a deep-fat fryer for 2 minutes or until golden brown. Drain on paper towels. Sprinkle the doughnuts liberally with sifted powdered sugar.

Sprinkle kirsch over the orange segments and toss lightly. Place each doughnut on a plate and arrange the orange segments around it. Serve at once.

Cinnamon Doughnuts

Five 2in doughnuts

½ quantity Doughnut recipe
2 teaspoons sugar
½ teaspoon ground cinnamon
Whipped cream with rum
5 strawberries

Prepare doughnuts as recipe and drain on paper towels.

Mix sugar and cinnamon together in a bag and lightly toss the doughnuts in it.

Pipe a large rosette of cream in the center of each doughnut and top with a strawberry. Serve at once.

Orange Syrup Cakes

Six 2in cakes

1 quantity Doughnut recipe made with ¼ cup semolina to replace 2 tablespoons of the flour. Omit the milk and add 1 tablespoon orange juice, grated rind of half an orange and ½ teaspoon ground cinnamon to the mixture.

Syrup
½ cup sugar
3 tablespoons orange juice
⅝ cup water

To serve
2 tablespoons Greek yogurt
Glazed Orange Peel Strands*

Divide the dough into six and lightly knead each piece into a 2in long fat bolster shape. Fry in a deep-fat fryer for 3 to 4 minutes until deep golden brown. Drain on paper towels and place the cakes in a small bowl.

To make the syrup, place the sugar, orange juice and water in a small saucepan and stir over a low heat until the sugar has dissolved. Increase heat and boil rapidly until the liquid has been reduced by half. Pour the syrup over the orange cakes and turn them over carefully. They can be served warm or cold.

To serve, spread a little yogurt on a small plate and place an Orange Syrup Cake on top. Sprinkle Glazed Orange Peel Strands on each and spoon any remaining syrup over the top.

To freeze
Orange Syrup Cakes can be frozen. When cold, remove from the syrup and place in a small freezer container. Allow to defrost slowly at room temperature.

Lemon Poppy Sticks
with Cranberry Cream

Five 1½in doughnuts

1 teaspoon grated lemon rind
2 teaspoons poppy seeds
*½ quantity Doughnut recipe (page 104),
    uncooked*
2 teaspoons Vanilla Sugar*
3 pieces semi-sweet chocolate
⅜ cup cream
3 tablespoons Cranberry Sauce*

Mix lemon rind and 1 teaspoon poppy seeds into
the dough. Divide the mixture into five pieces and
roll each into a 1½in sausage shape.

Fry doughnuts in a deep-fat fryer for 2 minutes
until golden brown on all sides. Drain on paper
towels.

Toss them in the reserved poppy seeds and
Vanilla Sugar, to coat.

Melt chocolate in a small bowl over hot water (or
in a microwave oven) and dip both ends of each
doughnut in chocolate; leave to set.

Whip the cream until stiff. Fold in 2 tablespoons
Cranberry Sauce.

Place a large swirl of cream on each serving plate,
top with a little Cranberry Sauce and place the
doughnut on one side.

Waffles

These crisp, wafer-like waffles are served with luscious sweet toppings. Make
them in advance, store in the freezer, and reheat under a hot broiler or in a toaster.
Prepare the topping before making the waffles.

Crispy Waffles

Twelve 2½in waffles

⅜ cup flour
Pinch of salt
1½ teaspoons baking powder
2 tablespoons sugar
1 egg, separated
1 tablespoon melted butter
⅝ cup milk
Butter for cooking

Sift flour, salt and baking powder into a medium
bowl. Add the sugar, beaten egg yolk, butter and
milk and beat until smooth.

Alternatively, place all these ingredients in a
blender or food processor and run machine until
batter is smooth.

Thoroughly butter a waffle iron and heat slowly
for 5 minutes. Beat egg white until stiff, and fold into
batter.

Pour 1 rounded tablespoon batter into center of
lower half of iron until it spreads to within 1in of the
edge.

Close and cook for about 1 minute, turning if
necessary, until the waffle is golden brown and
releases easily from the iron.

Serve the waffles hot with any of the following
toppings.

Ingredients, sauces, edible containers, etc
that are asterisked in the recipes on these
pages are given in detail on pages 147 to
156. For exact page numbers, refer to the
index at the end of the book.

Left Pentland Plum (page 109).

Lemon Waffles

Six 2½in waffles

½ quantity Crispy Waffles recipe (page 107)
1 teaspoon grated lemon rind

Stir lemon rind into batter and cook as directed.

Peach Melba

Six 2½in waffles

6 Lemon Waffles, as recipe
6 scoops Peach Sorbet (page 140)
A few drops almond extract
6 tablespoons Chantilly Cream (page 122)
2 tablespoons Cranberry Sauce*

Place each waffle on a small plate. Top with a scoop of Peach Sorbet.

Stir almond extract into the Chantilly Cream and swirl 1 tablespoon onto each sorbet. Top with a teaspoonful of Cranberry Sauce. Serve at once.

Banana and Chocolate Secrets

Six 2½in waffles

6 Crispy Waffles, as recipe (page 107)
3 large ripe bananas
6 teaspoons dark rum
6 tablespoons Hot Chocolate Sauce*
6 tablespoons whipped cream
12 Marzipan Leaves*

Place each waffle on a serving plate. Peel and halve the bananas, then slice them thinly and spread each half across one waffle, keeping a banana shape. Sprinkle rum over the bananas before covering with Hot Chocolate Sauce.

Pipe a line of cream along the top and decorate each with 2 Marzipan Leaves. Serve immediately.

Apricot Drop Scones

Six 2½in drop scones

Oil for greasing
½ quantity Crispy Waffle recipe (page 107)
3 fresh apricots (or 6 canned apricot halves)
¼ cup sugar
⅜ cup white wine
2 teaspoons brandy
6 tablespoons Chantilly Cream (page 122)
Chopped pistachio nuts

Lightly grease a griddle pan or heavy-based frying pan. Drop a soup spoon of batter onto the pan and cook 1 minute each side or until deep golden brown in color. Keep warm in a clean dish towel over a pan of hot water.

Halve apricots and remove pits (drain apricots if canned). Place sugar and wine in a small pan. Bring to a boil. Add apricot halves, reduce heat and simmer for 2 to 3 minutes. Remove apricots with a slotted spoon. Add brandy to the pan and cook syrup gently until it coats the back of the spoon.

Place an apricot half on each drop scone and drizzle some syrup over the fruit. Pipe small rosettes of Chantilly Cream around the edges of the scones and sprinkle pistachio nuts over the dessert.

Maple and Vanilla Waffles

Six 2½in waffles

6 Crispy Waffles, as recipe (page 107)
6 tiny scoops Vanilla Ice Cream (page 136)
4 tablespoons maple syrup
2 tablespoons Toasted Chopped Almonds*

Place each waffle on a serving plate. Place a scoop of ice cream on top and coat with maple syrup. Sprinkle nuts over syrup.

Note: Use a heart-shaped waffle iron if you have one.

Potato Pastry

Potato pastry, an Austrian speciality, makes a wonderfully soft crust for
sweet dishes.

Soft Potato Pastry

16 portions

¾lb large potatoes
2 tablespoons butter
3 tablespoons semolina
1 egg yolk
⅜-½ cup flour
1 teaspoon baking powder
¼ teaspoon salt

Scrub potatoes and bake in a hot oven until soft.
Scoop out the flesh and strain into a bowl. Add
butter, semolina, eggs, half the flour, the baking
powder and the salt. Beat ingredients together until
smooth. Gradually add sufficient flour to make a soft
dough. Knead lightly on a well-floured surface.
Cover pastry and leave in the refrigerator for 20
minutes.

Pentland Plums

6 covered plums

Oil for deep frying
6 small red plums
6 tablespoons marzipan
½ quantity Soft Potato Pastry recipe
¼ cup fresh white bread crumbs
2 teaspoons sherry
4 rounded tablespoons strained apricot purée,
  using fresh or dried apricots

Prepare a deep-fat fryer and heat oil to 370°F. Cut
two-thirds of the way around each plum and
remove the pits. Divide marzipan into six pieces
and use to fill the cavity in each plum.
   Remove pastry from refrigerator and lightly
knead on a well-floured surface until smooth.
Divide into six equal pieces, flatten and mold each
one round a plum to cover evenly. Roll in bread
crumbs, pressing them on lightly. Deep-fry plums 4
to 5 minutes until golden brown, turning them over
during cooking. Make sure that the fat is not too hot
or the outside will become too dark before the
plum is soft. Drain on paper towels and keep warm.
Serve with apricot sauce made by beating the sherry
into the apricot purée.

Mincemeat Curls

Six 3in curls

Oil for deep frying
½ quantity Soft Potato Pastry recipe
2 tablespoons sesame seeds
3 tablespoons mincemeat

To serve
6 Marzipan Leaves*
3 cherries, halved
Brandy Cream (page 122)

Prepare a deep-fat fryer and heat oil to 370°F. Lightly
knead the pastry until smooth on a well-floured
surface. Sprinkle sesame seeds lightly over this
surface and place pastry on top. Roll out pastry ¼in
thick and cut out six 3in circles.
   Place a teaspoon mincemeat in the center of each.
Brush the edges with water and fold pastry in half
over the filling. Seal edges and snip with scissors at
¼in intervals. Pull ends gently away from curve to
form a horseshoe.
   Deep-fry 2 to 3 minutes until golden brown.
Drain on paper towels and keep warm.
   To serve, decorate with a Marzipan Leaf and half a
cherry. Serve with Brandy Cream.

> Ingredients, sauces, edible containers, etc
> that are asterisked in the recipes on these
> pages are given in detail on pages 147 to
> 156. For exact page numbers, refer to the
> index at the end of the book.

Crêpes

Fine, lacy crêpes can be folded, rolled or formed into cones to make delicious containers for a variety of fillings. Make them in advance and store in the refrigerator or freezer.

Mini-Crêpes

Twenty 3in crêpes

¼ cup flour
Pinch of salt
1 egg, beaten
¼ cup plus 1 tablespoon milk
4 tablespoons water
1 tablespoon brandy
Butter or shortening for frying

Sift flour and salt together in a medium bowl. Mix egg, milk, water and brandy together and gradually beat into the flour to make a smooth batter. Alternatively, blend all the ingredients together until smooth.

Heat a small crêpe pan, griddle or heavy-based frying pan and brush with butter or shortening. Using a soup spoon place a spoonful of the batter in the pan and quickly and lightly spread out to a 3in circle with the back of the spoon. Repeat to make more mini-crêpes in the pan.

Fry for about one minute until set, then flip over and cook for 30 seconds until the second side is golden brown.

Slide the crêpes onto a plate placed over a pan of hot water and cook the remaining batter.

Variations
Each of the following recipes makes ten 3in crêpes.

Chocolate Crêpes
Sprinkle 1½ teaspoons cocoa powder and 1 teaspoon sugar over the surface of batter made with ½ quantity Mini-Crêpes recipe. Leave a few seconds before beating or blending in an electric blender

Orange Crêpes
Stir 2 teaspoons finely grated orange rind into batter made with ½ quantity Mini-Crêpes recipe.

Cinnamon Crêpes
Stir ½ teaspoon ground cinnamon into batter made with ½ quantity Mini-Crêpes recipe.

Coconut Crêpes
Stir 1 teaspoon shredded coconut into batter made with ½ quantity Mini-Crêpes recipe.

Freezing crêpes
Stack between pieces of waxed paper or freezer film. Place stack in a plastic bag and freeze for up to six weeks. Thaw at room temperature and reheat over hot water or in a microwave oven.

Right *Selection of crêpes, on black plate from left: Raspberries au Fromage (page 112); Chocolate and Nut (page 112); Banana with Butterscotch Sauce (page 113).*

Peaches and Praline Cream

Ten 3in filled crêpes

1 tablespoon orange juice
1 teaspoon sugar
1 peach, peeled, pitted and roughly chopped
1 tablespoon brandy
2 tablespoons Praline*
¼ cup heavy cream, lightly whipped
10 Mini-Crêpes, as recipe (page 110)

Heat the orange juice with the sugar in a small pan, add the peach and cook for 2 to 3 minutes. Strain through a strainer and reserve both fruit and juice. Stir the brandy into the juice and heat gently.

Fold the crushed Praline into the cream and divide between the crêpes. Place the blanched peach on the cream and fold the crêpes over. Sprinkle the orange juice mixture over the surface.

Raspberries au Fromage

Ten 3in filled crêpes

2 tablespoons sour cream
4 tablespoons softened cream cheese or strained
    cottage cheese
1 tablespoon powdered sugar
⅜ cup raspberries
10 Mini-Crêpes, as recipe (page 110)
1 tablespoon sifted powdered sugar

Beat the sour cream into the cheese until smooth. Beat in the powdered sugar.

Reserve a few raspberries for decoration and fold remainder into cheese mixture.

Fold the crêpes in half and fill with the raspberry cheese. Dust the top of the crêpes with sifted powdered sugar and serve with a few extra raspberries placed around them.

Successful cooking
When placing batter in the hot pan, use a quick, light-handed circular movement to ensure even spreading. Cook two or three crêpes together.

Chocolate and Nut

Ten 3in filled crêpes

1 egg yolk
2 teaspoons Vanilla Sugar*
2 teaspoons cornstarch
½ cup milk
2 squares chocolate, chopped
1 egg white
2 tablespoons sugar
2 tablespoons mixed nuts, finely chopped
2 tablespoons macaroons, coarsely crushed
3 tablespoons heavy cream
1 tablespoon brandy
10 Mini-Crêpes, as recipe (page 110)

Blend the egg yolk, Vanilla Sugar and cornstarch together in a small bowl. Bring the milk to a boil then stir into the egg yolk mixture. Pour into a small saucepan and cook, stirring, over a low heat, until the mixture thickens.

Meanwhile, melt the chocolate in a bowl placed over a pan of hot water, then stir into the custard.

Beat the egg white until stiff. Gradually beat in the sugar. Fit a small piping bag with a small star tube and fill with meringue.

Prepare a medium-hot broiler.

Mix the nuts, macaroons, cream and brandy into the chocolate custard and divide the mixture between the crêpes. Fold them over. Place on a baking sheet and pipe a pattern of meringue over the surface of each crêpe. Place under the broiler until lightly browned.

Walnut Ice Cream and Maple Syrup

Ten 3in filled crêpes

⅜ cup heavy cream, chilled
2 tablespoons brown sugar
2 tablespoons walnuts, very finely chopped
10 Chocolate Crêpes (page 110)
3 tablespoons maple syrup

Whip the cream with the brown sugar until it stands in soft peaks. Fold in the nuts then spoon into a shallow metal container, cover and place in the freezer or the top of the refrigerator until firm.

Prepare the crêpes, then place small scoops of the frozen walnut mixture in the center of each one. Fold the crêpes over. Trickle maple syrup over each. Serve at once.

Ground Almond and Curaçao

Ten 3in filled crêpes

10 Cinnamon Crêpes (page 110)
2 tablespoons sugar
2 tablespoons butter, softened
2 tablespoons ground almonds
1 teaspoon curaçao
Pat of clarified butter
2 tablespoons Toasted Flaked Almonds*
4 orange segments, pith and peel removed, chopped

Sauce
2 tablespoons orange curaçao
2 tablespoons brandy

Prepare the crêpes. Work the sugar, butter, ground almonds and curaçao together with a fork. Place down the center of the crêpes and fold over into rectangular parcels.

Heat the crêpe pan gently, then wipe around the inside with clarified butter. Place the crêpe parcels, seam-side down, in the pan.

To make the sauce, warm the curaçao and brandy in a ladle, ignite with a taper then pour over the crêpes. Serve immediately sprinkled with chopped orange segments and the Toasted Flaked Almonds.

To assist your timetable
Ground Almond and Curaçao filling can be prepared in advance. Wrap and keep in the refrigerator for up to 4 hours.

Keeping crêpes warm
Stack them on a plate over a pan of hot water and cover with a clean dish towel.

Banana with Butterscotch Sauce

Ten 3in filled crêpes

10 Orange Crêpes (page 110)
1 banana
2 teaspoons lemon juice
1 tablespoon butter
2 teaspoons brown sugar

Sauce
2 tablespoons butter
2 tablespoons soft brown sugar
3 tablespoons cream

Prepare the crêpes and keep warm.

Peel and slice the banana then sprinkle with lemon juice.

Melt the butter in a small non-stick frying pan then stir in the brown sugar and heat gently until the sugar has dissolved. Add the banana and cook on a low heat for 2 to 3 minutes.

Melt the butter for the sauce in a small non-stick saucepan. Stir in the sugar and heat gently until it has dissolved. Boil for 2 minutes, stirring constantly. Remove from the heat. Cool slightly then stir in the cream. Divide the banana mixture between the crêpes, then fold them over. Place on warmed plates and trickle the sauce over.

Rum and Pineapple

Ten 3in filled crêpes

10 Coconut Crêpes (page 110)
¼ cup peeled fresh pineapple, chopped
3 tablespoons dark rum
2 tablespoons sweet sherry
1 teaspoon cornstarch
1 teaspoon sugar
1 tablespoon powdered sugar

Prepare the crêpes and keep warm.

Marinate the pineapple in the rum and sherry in a bowl for 10 minutes. Blend cornstarch in a small saucepan with 1 tablespoon water then stir in the pineapple and liquid and sugar. Bring to a boil, stirring.

Divide the pineapple between the crêpes and fold them over. Place spoonfuls of the rum sauce on warmed plates and place the crêpes on top. Sprinkle with powdered sugar.

Windsor Slices

These delectable desserts, made from bread coated with egg and then fried, are a sweet variation on French toast. They taste especially good served with fruit or ice cream.

Windsor Slices

Six 2in circles

Three ¼in thick day-old slices white bread
1 egg
Pinch of cinnamon
⅜ cup white wine
3 tablespoons sugar
2 tablespoons butter

Using a 2in cookie cutter, cut out two circles from each slice of bread.

Beat egg, cinnamon, wine and 2 tablespoons sugar together in a bowl.

Heat butter in a small, heavy-based pan. Dip bread into egg mixture, lift out and fry 1 or 2 minutes on each side until golden brown. Toss bread in remaining sugar and serve hot with a choice of toppings.

Strawberry Cups

Six 2in cups

6 cooked Windsor Slices, as recipe
9 large, firm strawberries
2 tablespoons kirsch
1 egg white
¼ cup sugar

Prepare a medium-hot broiler. Place the Windsor Slices on an oven-proof plate.

Remove hulls from strawberries and cut each strawberry in half, lengthways. Place in a bowl and sprinkle with kirsch.

Beat egg white until stiff, then fold in the sugar. Place meringue in a piping bag fitted with a small star tube. Pipe a thick ring of meringue around the edge of each Windsor Slice. Place them under a medium-hot broiler until the meringue is lightly browned.

Arrange 3 strawberry halves in each and drizzle kirsch over. Serve at once.

Apricot Alaskas

Six 2in alaskas

6 Windsor Slices as recipe, but made with beer instead of wine and with bread cut into 2in squares
¼ cup dried apricots, soaked overnight
2 tablespoons brandy
2 tablespoons beer
2 egg whites
½ cup sugar
6 small scoops Vanilla Ice Cream (page 136)
18 small pieces angelica

Prepare a medium-hot broiler. Arrange the Windsor Slices on an oven-proof dish.

Blend the apricots, brandy and beer together in an electric blender until smooth. Divide between the fried slices.

Beat egg whites until thick; gradually beat in the sugar. Place meringue in a piping bag with a small star tube.

Arrange a scoop of ice cream on top of the purée and cover completely with swirls of meringue. Place alaskas under a medium-hot broiler until golden brown.

Serve the alaskas at once, each decorated with 3 pieces of angelica.

Right, from left Kumquat Fritters (page 116); Frosted Grapes (page 97); Fondue Fritters (page 116); Maraschino Cherry Fritters (page 116); 1¼in Rich Secret Dessert (page 117).

Fritters

Firm, tangy fruits are dipped in a light batter and deep-fried until crisp and golden in color. The coating helps to protect them from the heat and flavor of the oil.

Fruit Fritters

Twelve 1in fritters

Batter
¼ cup flour
Pinch of salt
¼ cup plus 1 tablespoon water
2 heaping tablespoons stiffly whipped egg white
Oil for deep frying
12 pieces of fruit, eg grapes, kumquats, apple pieces,
*   cherries, strawberries, damsons*

To make the batter, sift flour and salt into a bowl. Make a well in the center and add water. Beat until smooth. Leave batter to rest for 30 minutes. Just before using, carefully fold in the egg white with a metal spoon.

Prepare a deep-fat fryer and heat oil to 370°F. Dip pieces of fruit in the batter, shake off excess and place the fruit into the hot fat, only a few pieces at a time. Make sure the oil returns to the correct temperature before each new addition of fruit. Fry 3 to 4 minutes until golden brown, turning them over half way through cooking. Drain the fritters on paper towels and keep warm while frying the remaining pieces.

Fondue Fritters

Twelve 1in fritters

3 ounces blue cheese
1 quantity batter from Fruit Fritters recipe, using
*   rind and juice of one large orange in place of*
*   water*

To serve
3 tablespoons caraway seeds
About 24 Frosted Grapes (page 97)

Cut cheese into 12 squares and dip in batter. Deep-fry for 2 to 3 minutes until golden brown. Drain on paper towels, toss in caraway seeds to coat, and keep warm. Serve with Frosted Grapes.

Kumquat Fritters

Twelve 1in fritters

12 kumquats
1 quantity batter from Fruit Fritters recipe
2 tablespoons powdered sugar

Sauce
2 teaspoons brandy
Grated rind of ½ lemon
4 tablespoons warmed strained marmalade

Dip the kumquats in the batter and deep-fry for 1 minute, then remove from oil and re-dip in batter. Fry the fritters for 2 to 3 minutes until golden brown. Drain on paper towels and keep warm.

Sift powdered sugar over fritters before serving.

To make the sauce, stir the brandy and lemon rind into the strained marmalade in a small pan and heat through gently. Serve each fritter with a small spoonful of sauce.

Ginger Nuggets

Twelve 1in fritters

12 nuggets of preserved ginger in syrup
1 quantity batter from Fruit Fritters recipe
Sugar to coat

Ginger sauce
2 tablespoons syrup from the ginger jar
6 tablespoons thickly set Greek yogurt or sour cream

Dip nuggets of ginger in the batter. Deep-fry for 1 minute then remove and re-dip in the batter. Fry fritters for 2 to 3 minutes until golden brown. Drain on paper towels and keep warm.

Toss in sugar to coat.

To make the sauce, gradually add syrup to the yogurt or sour cream, stirring continuously. Serve each fritter with a spoonful of sauce.

Brandied Apple Fritters

Twelve 1in fritters

1½ small sweet, firm apples
3 tablespoons brandy
2 tablespoons granulated brown sugar
½ teaspoon ground cinnamon
1 quantity batter from Fruit Fritters recipe
Vanilla Sugar* or shredded coconut to coat

To serve
4 tablespoons whipped cream
Warmed, strained Cranberry Sauce*
12 Frosted Mint Leaves*

Halve, quarter, peel and core the apples. Cut each quarter into two pieces. Place brandy, brown sugar and cinnamon in a medium bowl, add apples and toss, to coat. Leave 20 minutes turning occasionally. Drain apples on paper towels. Reserve liquid.

Dip apples in batter and deep-fry 3 to 4 minutes until golden brown. Drain on paper towels and keep warm. Toss in Vanilla Sugar or shredded coconut, to coat.

Fold reserved liquid into whipped cream.

To serve, pour a little Cranberry Sauce over each fritter, decorate with a tiny Frosted Mint Leaf and add a little whipped cream.

Rich Secret Desserts

Twelve 1¼in portions

¾ cup marzipan
12 thick squares semi-sweet chocolate
1 quantity batter from Fruit Fritters recipe using
  rum in place of water

To serve
4 tablespoons whipped cream
1 tablespoon grated chocolate

Divide marzipan into 12 pieces and roll each piece into a square large enough to wrap around a piece of chocolate. Mould marzipan around chocolate to enclose.

Using tongs, dip the pieces in batter and deep-fry for 2 to 3 minutes until golden brown. Drain on paper towels and keep warm.

To serve, swirl a little cream on each plate and place a fritter to one side. Sprinkle a little grated chocolate over each fritter.

Caribbean Tipsies

Twelve 1½in fritters

12 fresh dates
¼ cup creamed coconut
1 quantity batter from Fruit Fritters recipe made
  with white wine in place of water

Coconut sauce
3 tablespoons flaked coconut
6 tablespoons thickly set yogurt

Split each date and remove the pits. Cut the creamed coconut into 12 equal pieces and use to stuff the dates. Dip dates in batter and deep-fry for 2 to 3 minutes until golden brown. Drain on paper towels and keep warm.

To make the sauce, stir 1 tablespoon flaked coconut into the yogurt. Serve each fritter with a spoonful of sauce. Sprinkle extra coconut over the fritters and sauce.

Strawberry Fritters

Twelve 1½in fritters

12 firm large strawberries
1 quantity batter from Fruit Fritters recipe
2 tablespoons powdered sugar

To serve
4 tablespoons whipped cream

Remove hulls from strawberries. Dip strawberries into the batter and deep-fry for 1 minute, then remove from fat and re-dip in batter. Return the fritters to the oil and fry for 2 to 3 minutes until golden brown. Drain on kitchen paper and keep warm.

Sift powdered sugar over fritters and serve with whipped cream.

Two into one
You can, if you wish, halve the quantities of fruit and other ingredients in these recipes and use the basic quantity of batter to make two batches (about six portions each) using different fruits.

Meringues, Macaroons

Meringues come in many guises, and can be flavored with chocolate, coffee and nuts; fillings provide all kinds of complementary tastes. Macaroons are rich almond cookies.

French Meringue

This simple combination of egg white and sugar can be shaped into shells, and vacherins for combining with exotic ingredients.

French Meringue

About 10 portions

1 egg white
¼ cup sugar or soft brown sugar

Make sure that no egg yolk is present. Place the white in a dry grease-free bowl, preferably copper or a mixer bowl. Beat slowly at first then on high speed until the foam is stiff. Beat in half the sugar until the meringue is stiff and shiny. Sprinkle the remaining sugar over and fold in gently with a spatula or metal spoon, cutting through the mixture and turning it over until all the sugar is mixed in.

Shape or pipe on to non-stick baking parchment on a baking sheet. Dry out in a very cool oven or warming drawer, 200°F.

Chocolate
Add 1 ounce grated semi-sweet chocolate with the second half of the sugar.

Hazelnut
Fold 2 tablespoons Toasted Chopped Hazelnuts* with the sugar. Shape and dry out the meringue before the oil in the nuts makes the foam collapse.

Almond
Fold in 2 tablespoons ground almonds and one drop of almond extract.

Coffee
Mix 1 teaspoon instant coffee or finely ground filter coffee with the sugar before folding in. The meringue is attractively speckled.

Meringue Discs

Sixteen 2in discs

Cut non-stick baking parchment to fit a baking sheet and draw 2in circles a little apart. Fit a nylon piping bag with a ¼in plain piping tube and fill with French Meringue, flavored as appropriate. Starting from the center, pipe meringue in the circles. Bake in a very cool oven, 200°F for about 1 hour until the discs will lift off easily. Cool, then store in an airtight box. Use for the following recipes.

Previous pages, clockwise from left *Apricot and Hazelnut Vacherin (right) surrounded by 1½in Orange and Walnut Whirls (page 125); Rose Cream Meringues (page 122); Macaroons (page 129) surrounded by Chocolate Mint (page 124) and Mocha Meringues (page 124) and Coconut Macaroons (page 129); Valentine Pavlova (page 128); Walnut Macaroons (page 129); Strawberry Meringue Gâteau (opposite).*

Apricot and Hazelnut Vacherins

Four 2in vacherins

2 tablespoons dried apricots
2 tablespoons clear honey
¼ cup boiling water
¼ cup heavy cream
8 Meringue Discs with hazelnut flavoring (above)
6 pistachio nuts, chopped

Blend apricots and honey together with the boiling water; leave 15 minutes.

Beat the cream until stiff. Beat in half the apricot purée and use to sandwich the meringues. Top each vacherin with chopped pistachio nuts and serve with the remaining apricot sauce poured over.

Thin the sauce with a little more honey if it is too thick to pour.

Raspberry Tie-Ups

Four 2in raspberry tie-ups

A drop of green food coloring
2 tablespoons white marzipan
12 raspberries
1 quantity Chantilly Cream filling (page 122)
8 Meringue Discs with almond flavoring (opposite)

Knead a drop of coloring into the marzipan, roll out and trim to a 9 × 1in strip. Cut into four strips ¼in wide.

Crush 8 raspberries and mix into the cream. Sandwich the discs with this cream filling and place a raspberry on top of each.

Cut one strip of marzipan in half and attach underneath a filled vacherin at opposite sides. Tie over the top of the raspberry. Repeat with remaining meringues.

Vacherin Chantilly with Raspberry Sauce

Four 2in vacherins

½ cup raspberries
2 tablespoons sugar
1 tablespoon kirsch
8 Meringue Discs with almond flavoring (opposite),
*   topped with a sprinkling of flaked almonds before*
*   baking*
1 quantity Chantilly Cream filling (page 122)
1 teaspoon powdered sugar, sifted

Cook raspberries gently in a small saucepan until the juice runs. Press through a nylon strainer; mix purée with sugar and kirsch. Spread the purée on four small serving plates.

Sandwich the Meringue Discs with Chantilly Cream filling and dredge with powdered sugar. Place one in the center of each plate.

Beating egg whites
Egg whites will not beat if there is any grease present. It is best to wash the bowl and beaters in hot soapy water and dry them thoroughly with a clean, dry cloth before starting.

Strawberry Meringue Gâteau

Four to five 4in portions

½ quantity French Meringue with hazelnut
*   flavoring (opposite)*
2 squares chocolate
½ cup heavy cream
1 tablespoon Grand Marnier
½ teaspoon finely grated orange rind
8 strawberries, sliced
1 tablespoon red currant jelly
1 pistachio nut, chopped

Spread or pipe the meringue in two 4in marked circles on non-stick baking parchment. Dry out in a cool oven, 200°F, for 1 hour or until circles will lift easily off the parchment.

Melt the chocolate in a small bowl over hot water and spread over the base of one meringue layer.

Beat the cream until stiff, then whip in the Grand Marnier and orange rind. Spread half over the chocolate meringue base on a serving plate.

Arrange about one-third of the strawberries on the top meringue circle and one-third on the cream. Sandwich together, pipe stars of remaining cream on top and decorate with the chopped pistachio nut. Melt the red currant jelly gently and use to glaze the strawberries. Arrange the remaining sliced strawberries on the plate around the gâteau with points outwards. Leave for at least ½ hour for the meringue to soften slightly before serving.

Almond Meringue Towers

Nine 2in towers

1 quantity French Meringue with almond flavoring
*   (opposite)*
1 quantity Chocolate Cream filling (page 122)
1 tablespoon powdered sugar, sifted
Pink Marzipan Daisies*

Fit a nylon piping bag with a ¼in plain piping tube. Fill with meringue and pipe nine 2in, nine 1½in and nine small beads on to non-stick baking parchment. Dry out in a cool oven, 200°F, for about 1 hour until meringues easily lift off the parchment.

Beat Chocolate Cream until thick, then pipe with a small star tube to layer the meringues. Leave ½ hour before serving to soften slightly then sprinkle with powdered sugar, and decorate each with 6 tiny pink Marzipan Daisies.

Mini Meringue Shells

Twenty 1in shells; 10 portions

Cover a baking sheet with non-stick baking parchment. Take a heaped teaspoonful of flavored French Meringue (page 120), smooth the top to form a dome then use another teaspoon to scoop the meringue on to the parchment. Shape an even number then dry out for about 1 hour until they easily lift off the parchment. Use vanilla, chocolate, coffee or hazelnut flavored meringue, according to the fillings.

Fillings

¼ cup heavy cream

Chantilly Cream
Beat the cream with 1 teaspoon sugar and a few drops of real vanilla extract.

Chocolate Cream
Break up 1 ounce chocolate, place in a bowl and heat in a microwave oven or gently in a small saucepan with the cream. Cool, chill, then add 1 tablespoon dark rum.

Coffee Cream
Dissolve 1 teaspoon instant coffee in 1 teaspoon boiling water. Beat into the cream.

Praline Cream
Beat 2 teaspoons Praline* into the cream.

Orange Cream
Beat 1 teaspoon finely grated orange rind into the cream. Add a tiny drop of orange food coloring, if desired.

Lemon Cream
Beat 1 teaspoon finely grated lemon rind into the cream.

Liqueur or Brandy Cream
Beat 1 tablespoon Tia Maria, Grand Marnier, Cointreau, curaçao, crème de menthe or brandy into the cream.

Rose Cream Meringues

Five 2in filled meringues

1 quantity Chantilly Cream filling
1 teaspoon rose water
10 Mini Meringue Shells, each sprinkled with a
*   pinch of Colored Crystals* before baking*
5 Frosted Rose Petals*

Beat Chantilly Cream filling with rose water. Pipe between 2 shells, arrange on a plate and decorate each with a Frosted Rose Petal.

Meringue Belle Hélène

Five 2in filled meringues

2 ounces semi-sweet chocolate, chopped
½ teaspoon instant coffee
3 tablespoons water
2 teaspoons corn syrup
1 small ripe pear
1 tablespoon kirsch
Five 1in cubes Vanilla Ice Cream (page 136)
10 Mini Meringue Shells

Place the chocolate, coffee, water and corn syrup in a small saucepan. Heat gently until the chocolate has melted, then simmer for 2 minutes.

Peel the pear, cut into five wedges and turn these in the kirsch to prevent browning.

To serve, sandwich a cube of ice cream between 2 Mini Meringue Shells, place a pear wedge on top and pour hot chocolate sauce over.

Quantities
To make ten 1in flavored meringue shells, reduce the flavoring ingredients by half and add to half the French Meringue mixture.

Right, clockwise from top left *Orange and Walnut Whirls (page 125); 1in Meringue Stars (page 125); Orange and Walnut Whirls.*

Chocolate Chip Meringues

Five 2in filled meringues

10 Mini Meringue Shells (page 122) made with
*   chocolate-flavored French Meringue (page 120)*
1 quantity Orange Cream filling (page 122)
1 tablespoon Cointreau
A few drops orange food coloring
Shreds of orange rind, thinly cut

Sandwich the Mini Meringue Shells with Orange
Cream filling, beaten until stiff with Cointreau and
tinted pale orange with food coloring.

    Sprinkle shreds of orange rind over the cream.

Mocha Meringues

Five 2in filled meringues

10 Mini Meringue Shells (page 122) made with
*   coffee-flavored French Meringue (page 120)*
1 quantity Chocolate Cream filling (page 122)
5 chocolate coffee bean candies

Sandwich the Mini Meringue Shells with Chocolate
Cream filling and top each with a chocolate coffee
bean candy.

    Place in petits fours cases (optional).

Jamaica Meringues

Five 2in filled meringues

2 tablespoons raisins
3 tablespoons dark rum
2 tablespoons sponge cake crumbs
10 Mini Meringue Shells (page 122) made with
*   coffee-flavored French Meringue (page 120)*
1 tablespoon powdered sugar
5 pineapple pieces, cut very small

Chop raisins finely and soak in the rum for 1 hour.
Mix in the cake crumbs, then sandwich the Mini
Meringue Shells with this filling.

    Sprinkle the powdered sugar over them and
decorate each with a tiny piece of pineapple.

Hazelnut Chantilly Meringues

Five 2in filled meringues

10 Mini Meringue Shells (page 122) made with
*   hazelnut-flavored French Meringue (page 120)*
1 quantity Chantilly Cream filling (page 122)
2 squares semi-sweet chocolate
1 teaspoon honey

Sandwich the Mini Meringue Shells with Chantilly
Cream filling.

    Melt the chocolate in a small bowl over hot water
with the honey. Spoon into a cone of waxed paper,
snip off the point and pipe zig-zags of chocolate
over the meringues and cream. Leave to set, then
place in petits fours cases.

Marnier Meringues

Five 2in filled meringues

1 quantity Liqueur Cream filling with Grand
*   Marnier flavor (page 122)*
10 Mini Meringue Shells (page 122) made with
*   hazelnut-flavored French Meringue (page 120)*
5 mandarin orange segments

After whipping, pipe Liqueur Cream filling between
5 pairs of Mini Meringue Shells. Decorate each
serving with a mandarin orange segment.

Chocolate Mint Meringues

Five 2in filled meringues

A few drops green food coloring
1 quantity Liqueur Cream filling (page 122) with
*   crème de menthe*
10 Mini Meringue Shells (page 122) made with
*   chocolate-flavored French Meringue (page 120)*
5 Frosted Mint Leaves*

Beat the food coloring into the Liqueur Cream
filling to tint pale green. Pipe between pairs of Mini
Meringue Shells and place in paper cases.

    Decorate each with a tiny Frosted Mint Leaf.

Meringue Cuite

This is the easiest meringue to make. It does not need baking, unless it is used for a tall basket and can be flavored, tinted with food coloring and piped in shapes to form the base for desserts.

Meringue Cuite

1 egg white
6 tablespoons powdered sugar

Place the egg white and powdered sugar in a small, very clean bowl. Place bowl over a small saucepan of boiling water and remove from the heat. Beat on high speed, with an electric beater if possible, until the meringue is very stiff and stands in peaks.

Color and flavor as in the following recipes, then pipe or shape onto non-stick baking parchment. Leave in a warm dry place overnight to dry out.

Meringue Stars

Use these for topping mousses and decorating desserts. Sandwich together with Chocolate Cream (page 122) or Rich Butter Cream*.

Eighteen 1in meringue stars

1 quantity Meringue Cuite
A drop each of yellow, green, pink and lavender food colorings

Divide the stiffly beaten meringue into five cups. Add a drop of food coloring to each one, leaving one white.

Fit a nylon piping bag with a star tube and pipe stars of meringue onto non-stick baking parchment. Start with white, then fill bag with yellow then green meringue to avoid washing the bag and tube. Wash and dry the bag and tube before filling with pink then lavender meringue.

Dry out overnight in a warm dry place then lift off the parchment and store in an airtight tin or plastic box.

Orange and Walnut Whirls

Makes six 1½in whirls

½ quantity Meringue Cuite
1 teaspoon finely grated orange rind
1 drop orange food coloring
6 walnut halves

Bases

2 tablespoons butter
2 tablespoons powdered sugar
½ teaspoon instant coffee
1 teaspoon boiling water
2 tablespoons crushed graham crackers
2 tablespoons chopped walnuts
4 tablespoons cream cheese
1 teaspoon grated orange rind
1 teaspoon orange juice
1 teaspoon powdered sugar

Beat meringue with orange rind and coloring and pipe six 1½in whirls onto non-stick baking parchment. Place a walnut half on each and leave overnight to dry out.

Cream butter and powdered sugar in a small bowl until soft and fluffy. Dissolve instant coffee in boiling water and add to butter mixture. Add the graham cracker crumbs to the bowl with the walnuts. Form into six balls then flatten with a knife.

Beat cream cheese with orange rind, juice and powdered sugar. Divide between the bases and place a meringue on each.

Keeping meringues
Though meringues will freeze successfully, they need protecting in sturdy boxes. It is easier to store them just in the cupboard as they have a long life when unfilled.

Pavlova

This meringue with a soft center, a native of Australia and New Zealand, is often preferred to the crisper French type. It can be used in most of the same ways. Because it is cooked at a slightly higher temperature than French meringue, Pavlova is more creamy colored. It stores well and will keep in an airtight tin or plastic box for up to two weeks. Pavlova needs to be beaten very stiffly, preferably with an electric beater.

Australian Pavlova

For 10 to 12 portions

1 large egg white
6 tablespoons powdered sugar
1/2 teaspoon vinegar
1/2 teaspoon vanilla extract
1/2 teaspoon cornstarch

Prepare a cool oven at 300°F. Line a baking sheet with non-stick baking parchment.

Beat egg white until stiff; gradually beat in all of the sugar at top speed. Blend vinegar, vanilla extract and cornstarch together in a small bowl and beat into the meringue. The meringue should be very stiff and glossy. Shape or pipe on to the baking parchment.

Reduce oven heat to very cool at 250°F, and bake pavlova for the time given in each recipe. Leave to cool in the oven.

Passion Fruit Pavlovas

Five 2in Pavlovas

1/2 quantity Australian Pavlova mixture
5 tablespoons Diplomat Cream*
1 passion fruit
15 pink Marzipan Hearts* for decoration

Prepare a cool oven at 300°F.

Draw five 2in circles on non-stick baking parchment and pipe meringue in the circles. Pipe a wall of stars around each. Place in the oven, turn down the heat to very cool at 250°F, and leave for 40 minutes. Turn off the oven and allow pavlovas to cool in oven.

To serve, place Diplomat Cream in a small bowl. Cut the passion fruit in half and add fruit to the bowl; mix well then divide between the pavlovas. Decorate with tiny pink Marzipan Hearts.

Coffee Meringue Fingers

Six 2½in fingers

2 teaspoons instant coffee
1/2 teaspoon water
1/2 quantity Australian Pavlova mixture
Finely chopped walnuts
1/4 quantity Rich Butter Cream* flavored with 2 teaspoons Tia Maria
2 ounces semi-sweet chocolate

Heat oven to 300°F.

Dissolve coffee in the water and beat into the pavlova mixture. Fit a nylon piping bag with a 1/2in star piping tube, fill with pavlova mixture and pipe 2½in bars in a zig-zag action like a corkscrew on non-stick baking parchment. Sprinkle with finely chopped walnuts and place in the oven. Reduce heat immediately to very cool (250°F) and leave to dry out for 1/2 hour. Turn off the heat and leave pavlova in the oven until cold.

Sandwich pavlova fingers in pairs with Rich Butter Cream. Melt chocolate in a small bowl over hot water and dip the ends of the meringues in the chocolate. Leave to set on non-stick baking parchment, then store in a tin.

Right, from top Raspberry Tie-Up (page 121); 2in Almond Meringue Towers (page 121); Apricot and Hazelnut Vacherin (page 120).

Valentine Pavlovas

Five 3in pavlovas

1/2 quantity Australian Pavlova mixture (page 126)
*2 tablespoons Praline**

Filling
1 cup raspberries
1 teaspoon sugar
1/4 cup heavy cream
*10 tiny Frosted Flowers**

Draw five heart shapes 3in long on non-stick baking parchment. Heat oven to 300°F.

Make the pavlova mixture as directed and fold in the Praline when stiff. Work quickly as the Praline will soften the foam. Fit a nylon piping bag with a medium-sized star tube and fill with 3 heaping tablespoons of the mixture. Spread remaining mixture in the heart shapes, then pipe shells around. Place in the oven, turn down the heat to very cool at 250°F, and leave for 40 minutes. Turn off the oven and allow the pavlovas to cool.

Cook raspberries until the juice is released. Press through a nylon strainer to make a purée; add sugar, then cool. Beat cream until stiff, gradually beat in the purée, then spread in each pavlova. Decorate each dessert with Frosted Flowers.

Apricot Pavlovas

Six 2½in pavlovas

1/4 cup heavy cream
2 teaspoons Amaretto liqueur
6 round Australian Pavlovas (page 126) with piped sides
3 fresh apricots or 6 canned apricot halves
*1 tablespoon Apricot Glaze**

Whip the cream with the liqueur and place a teaspoonful in each pavlova.

If fresh apricots are used, cut in halves and poach for 4 minutes in sugar syrup in a saucepan. Drain, dry on paper towels and cool. Place one half in each pavlova. Brush with warmed Apricot Glaze.

Citrus Meringue Bar

One 5 × 3in bar; 4–5 slices

1/2 quantity Australian Pavlova mixture (page 126)

Filling
1 egg yolk
2 tablespoons sugar
Finely grated rind and juice of 1/2 lemon
2 tablespoons heavy cream
5 mandarin orange segments
5 black grapes
*6 Marzipan Leaves**

Prepare a cool oven at 300°F. Draw two oblongs, each 5 × 3in on non-stick baking parchment.

Place the meringue in a piping bag fitted with a large star tube and pipe about three-quarters of the meringue into each oblong. Pipe shells around the edge of one to form a case. Place meringue in the oven and immediately reduce temperature to very cool at 250°F. Leave to dry out for 35 minutes then turn the oven off and leave until oven is cold.

To make the filling, beat egg yolk, sugar, rind and juice of 1 lemon in a small bowl over a saucepan of boiling water until the mixture is thick and leaves a trail when the beater is lifted. Remove bowl from the heat and beat the mixture until cool. In another small bowl beat the cream until thick then fold into the lemon mixture.

Spread half the filling on each pavlova layer. Arrange mandarin orange segments over top layer; cut the grapes in half, remove the seeds and arrange with the oranges. Sandwich the layers together. Decorate with Marzipan Leaves. Assemble at least 1 hour before serving to make the dessert easy to cut. Cut into five slices.

Ingredients, sauces, edible containers, etc that are asterisked in the recipes on these pages are given in detail on pages 147 to 156. For exact page numbers, refer to the index at the end of the book.

Macaroons

Macaroons are sweet confections of minced or ground nuts. Almonds are traditional, but walnuts, hazelnuts and coconut all make delicious sweet, chewy cookies. In Italy, a proportion of bitter almonds is added, while Austrian macaroons often contain hazelnuts, walnuts or chocolate. Rice flour is sometimes included to improve the texture. Macaroons are usually piped onto rice paper and decorated with a split almond or a glacé cherry. When the mixture is used for gâteaux, it is best to pipe it onto non-stick baking parchment.

Macaroons

About thirty-six 1in macaroons

½ cup sugar
¼ cup ground almonds
1 teaspoon ground rice
1 large egg white
1 drop almond extract
Sheet of rice paper
About 36 split almonds

Mix sugar, almonds and rice in a medium bowl. Add egg white and almond extract and beat with a wooden spoon or electric beater until the mixture is thick. Leave for 15 minutes.

Place a sheet of rice paper on a baking sheet, shiny side down. Prepare a moderate oven (350°F).

Beat the macaroon mixture again until very thick and white, then place in a nylon piping bag fitted with a ½in plain tube. Pipe in 1in rounds (or as directed in the recipes that follow), leaving room for them to spread. Place a split almond in the center of each. Bake for about 20 minutes until set and pale golden brown.

Fingers

Pipe the macaroon mixture in 2in lengths, using a nylon piping bag fitted with a ½in plain tube.

Storage of macaroons
Store macaroons in tins or airtight plastic boxes. They will keep for up to 4 weeks. The macaroons will soften slightly but the taste will develop.

Hazelnut Macaroons

Toast ¼ cup hazelnuts in a hot oven until browned. Cool, then slip off the skins and grind the hazelnuts finely in a blender or food processor, or chop them very finely.

Follow the recipe for Almond Macaroons, but replace the ground almonds with the hazelnuts, adding 1 drop of vanilla extract instead of the almond extract. Place a hazelnut in the center of each macaroon.

Walnut Macaroons

Replace hazelnuts with untoasted, chopped walnuts.

Coconut Macaroons

Follow the recipe for Almond Macaroons, but replace the ground almonds with shredded coconut and omit the almond extract. Top with pieces of glacé cherry.

Hazelnut Macaroon Deckers

Three 2in deckers

Six 2in Hazelnut Macaroons (without whole nuts on top)
Three 2in Meringue Discs (page 120)
1 quantity Liqueur Cream filling (page 122), flavored with orange curaçao
Meringue Stars (page 125) flavored with ½ teaspoon finely grated orange rind

Layer a Hazelnut Macaroon, a French Meringue, then another Hazelnut Macaroon with Liqueur Cream. Leave to soften for ½ hour before serving, and decorate each with a star.

Iced Desserts

Iced desserts include simple ice creams, spectacular gâteaux and bombes, tangy water ices, granitas and smooth sorbets. They can all be made in a freezer, or the ice-making compartment of a refrigerator.

Ice Creams

These include smooth, creamy ices made from a mixture of rich cream and fruit purée, moscovites, which have a softly set, mousse-like texture, and classic custard-based ice creams flavored and shaped to make all kinds of desserts.

Fruit Purée Ice Cream

This recipe is suitable for raspberries, strawberries, gooseberries, cranberries, mulberries, black currants, red currants, peaches, apricots, nectarines, mangosteen, melon, chestnut, apples, pears, oranges, lemons, limes, bananas and cherries. Fresh or canned fruit may be used.

1 pint; 8 portions

1 cup fruit
Sugar to taste
1 egg, separated
1/4 cup powdered sugar
1 cup heavy cream

Prepare the fruit: blend in an electric blender, and strain, raw berry fruit, apricots, peaches and nectarines, or cook the harder fruits in a little water or wine before blending, straining and chilling. Add sugar to taste.

Beat the egg white until it forms soft peaks. Gradually beat in the powdered sugar then the egg yolk. Fold in the fruit purée and pour the mixture into a large freezer container. Freeze for 1 hour or until the ice cream is firm 1in around the edge. Quickly beat the mixture with an electric beater until it is smooth, or turn it into a chilled food processor bowl and process until smooth. Beat the cream until it forms soft peaks. Fold into the half-set ice cream and return it to the freezer. Freeze for 1 hour then repeat the beating. Cover with foil and freeze until firm.

Before serving, place in the refrigerator for about 45 minutes to soften slightly.

Apple and Ginger Ice Cream

1 pint; 6 to 8 portions

1 cup prepared cooking apples
2 tablespoons syrup from jar of preserved ginger
Knob of butter
1 quantity Fruit Purée Ice Cream (using the apples to make the purée)
2 pieces preserved ginger
6 teaspoons ginger syrup

Peel, core and slice the apples. Simmer with ginger syrup and butter until soft. Beat until smooth. Cool, then chill.

Proceed as basic recipe.

Finely chop ginger and stir in after final beating.

To serve, scoop into small glasses and spoon a little ginger syrup over each portion.

Red Cherry Ice Cream

1 pint; 8 portions
2 cups canned red cherries
2 tablespoons maraschino de cuisine
1 quantity Fruit Purée Ice Cream (using cherries for purée)

Remove any pits from the cherries. Blend in an electric blender, strain, stir in the liqueur and chill. Proceed as basic recipe.

Previous pages, from left *Single scoops of ice cream: Pina Colada Ice Cream (page 136); Raspberry Moscovite (page 134); Chocolate Chip and Raisin (page 137); Gooseberry and Walnut Ice Cream (opposite); Blue Cheese Moscovite (page 134).*

Gooseberry and Walnut Ice Cream

1 pint; 8 portions

1 cup gooseberries
1 head elderflower (optional)
Juice of ½ orange
1 quantity Fruit Purée Ice Cream (using gooseberries for purée)
Green food coloring
2 tablespoons shelled walnuts

To serve
Chopped walnuts

Simmer gooseberries with elderflower (if used) and orange juice until soft. Strain gooseberries, cool, then chill the purée.

Proceed as basic recipe tinting ice cream with food coloring as required.

Chop walnuts finely and fold in after final beating.

Sprinkle each portion with chopped walnuts before serving.

Chestnut and Rum Ice Cream

1 pint; 8 portions

4 tablespoons sweetened chestnut purée
2 tablespoons dark rum
1 quantity Fruit Purée Ice Cream, omitting egg yolk and using only half the powdered sugar

To serve
8 Chocolate Cases*
Pieces of marron glacé

Beat chestnut purée with the rum. Fold the meringue mixture into the purée. Proceed as basic recipe.

Cube and serve in Chocolate Cases, decorated with pieces of marron glacé.

Red Berry Yogurt Ice Cream

1 pint; 8 portions

1 cup raspberries, strawberries, loganberries or mulberries
1 quantity Fruit Purée Ice Cream, with 1 cup thick-set plain yogurt instead of cream

Follow basic recipe, using the red berries to make the purée, but reserving 8 berries for decoration.

Substitute yogurt for the cream and gently fold in. Proceed as basic recipe.

Serve small scoops in sherry glasses and top each portion with a berry.

Soft-Set Moscovite

Suitable for soft fruits, plums, damsons, greengages, red and black currants, peaches, nectarines, apricots, melon, cherries, citrus fruits, kiwi fruit and mango.

1¼ pints; 10 portions

2 teaspoons powdered gelatin
1 cup fruit purée
2 egg whites
¼ cup sugar
1 cup light cream

Place gelatin with 2 tablespoons warm water in a small bowl. Place bowl over a pan of hot water until gelatin has melted. Cool. Stir into fruit purée. Place the purée in the refrigerator and chill for 15 minutes until softly set. Beat mixture.

Beat egg whites until they form soft peaks, then beat in the sugar and fold meringue into the purée. Stir in the cream. Place mixture in a freezer container. Cover and freeze at least 2 hours. No beating is required.

Place moscovites in the refrigerator for about ½ hour before serving, to soften slightly.

Moscovites
These are a cross between a fruit ice and a sorbet. Not as rich as ice creams, or as stiffly frozen as sorbets, they need gelatin in order to set.

Raspberry Moscovite

1¼ pints; 10 portions

1 quantity Soft-Set Moscovite recipe (page 133)
using 1 cup raspberry purée, strained
6 tablespoons Framboise Eau de Vie liqueur
½ cup raspberries

To serve
Raspberry Sauce*
10 raspberries

Follow basic recipe, stirring the liqueur in with the purée.

Chop the raspberries and fold in just before placing the ice cream in the freezer container.

Serve with Raspberry Sauce, topped with a raspberry.

Peach or Apricot Moscovite

About 1¼ pints; 10 portions

1 quantity Soft-Set Moscovite recipe (page 133)
using 1 cup peach or apricot purée
4 tablespoons apricot brandy

Decoration
Toasted Flaked Almonds*

Make as for basic recipe, stirring the apricot brandy in with the purée.

Serve in tiny scoops or cubes in sherry glasses. Decorate with the Toasted Flaked Almonds.

Banana and Rum Moscovite

About 1¼ pints; 10 portions

1 quantity Soft-Set Moscovite recipe (page 133)
replacing fruit purée with 4 large ripe bananas
2 tablespoons sugar
6 tablespoons white rum
2 tablespoons lemon juice

To serve
10 Chocolate Cases*

Mash the bananas with the sugar, while the melted gelatin is cooling, and mix them with the rum and lemon juice. Stir gelatin quickly into bananas, then continue with basic recipe.

Serve in tiny scoops in Chocolate Cases.

Blue Cheese Moscovite

Eight 1in cubes

1 cup medium-fat soft curd cheese
2 tablespoons orange juice
Grated rind of ½ an orange
½ quantity Soft-Set Moscovite recipe (page 133),
without purée. Replace the light cream with
1 cup thick-set plain yogurt.
¼ cup (2 ounces) blue cheese

To serve
Coupelles (page 65)

Beat the curd cheese until smooth; add orange juice and orange rind. Stir into basic recipe instead of the purée.

Roughly chop the blue cheese and fold it into the mixture just before placing in a shallow freezer container.

Serve in small chilled dishes with Coupelles.

Ginger and Yogurt Moscovite

¾ pint; 5 portions

½ quantity Soft-Set Moscovite recipe (page 133)
replacing the cream with ½ cup thick-set plain
yogurt
½ cup apple purée
2 pieces preserved ginger
4 ginger snaps, finely crushed

Decoration
Crushed ginger snaps

Make basic recipe using apple purée and stirring in yogurt instead of the cream. Finely chop the ginger and fold in with the crushed cookies just before placing the mixture in a freezer container.

Scoop the moscovite into small, chilled glasses and sprinkle the remaining crushed ginger snaps on top. Serve immediately.

Right, from left *Granita de Menthe (page 141) served in a sherry glass; Lemon Water Ice (page 141); Black Currant Sorbet with Champagne (page 140).*

Vanilla Ice Cream

1 pint; 8 portions

1 vanilla bean
1¾ cups light cream
3 egg yolks
⅜ cup sugar
1⅛ cups heavy cream

Place the vanilla bean and light cream in a heavy-based saucepan and heat slowly to just below boiling point. Remove from the heat and leave to cool. Remove the vanilla bean and reheat the cream to simmering point.

Place egg yolks and sugar in a bowl and beat until pale and creamy. Stir in the light cream. Return mixture to the saucepan and stir over a low heat until the mixture thickens and coats the back of the spoon. Do not boil or the mixture will separate. Pour custard into a large bowl and stir occasionally until cool.

Beat the heavy cream until it forms soft peaks. Fold into the custard mixture and place in a large freezer container. Chill, then place in freezer and leave for 1 hour. Remove and beat the mixture with a beater, or in the chilled bowl of a food processor until smooth. Repeat after a further hour. Stir in the flavoring. Cover and freeze a further 2 hours or more.

Put in the refrigerator for about 45 minutes to soften slightly before serving.

Almond Ice Cream

¾ pint; 6 portions

2 tablespoons ratafias
1in piece angelica
½ quantity Vanilla Ice Cream recipe
2 tablespoons Amaretto liqueur

To serve
Hot Chocolate Sauce*

Roughly chop ratafias. Finely chop angelica and fold into the ice cream after the final beating with the ratafias and Amaretto. Finish as for basic recipe. Serve in sherry glasses with Hot Chocolate Sauce.

Chocolate Ice Cream

¾ pint; 6 portions

½ quantity Vanilla Ice Cream recipe
4 ounces semi-sweet chocolate
2 tablespoons milk

To serve
6 teaspoons orange, mint or coffee liqueur

Follow the basic recipe until the custard thickens and remove from heat. Finely chop the chocolate and stir into hot custard until melted. Stir in the milk. Finish as basic recipe.

Serve tiny scoops in small glasses and top each portion with a teaspoon of liqueur.

Pina Colada Ice Cream

1 pint; 8 portions

½ quantity Vanilla Ice Cream recipe
¼ cup coconut cream
¼ cup pineapple
2 tablespoons Malibu liqueur

To serve
16 Langues des Chats (page 64)
8 maraschino cherries with stalks

Finely chop coconut cream and place with the cream from the basic recipe in a saucepan. Follow Vanilla Ice Cream recipe until the final beating. Finely chop pineapple. Fold into ice cream with the Malibu liqueur.

Serve with Langues des Chats, and top each portion with a cherry.

Cassata Ice Cream

¾ pint; 6 portions

¼ cup glacé cherries
2 tablespoons crystallized ginger
½ quantity Vanilla Ice Cream recipe
2 tablespoons chopped pistachio nuts
2 tablespoons Maraschino liqueur

To serve
6 Chocolate Cases*

Finely chop the cherries and ginger and fold into the ice cream with the nuts and liqueur after the final beating. Finish as for the basic recipe.

Serve in Chocolate Cases.

Brown Bread Ice Cream

¾ pint; 6 portions

½ quantity Vanilla Ice Cream recipe, using
chilled condensed milk instead of
cream
4 tablespoons butter
2 tablespoons sugar
¼ cup fresh brown bread crumbs
2 tablespoons Tia Maria

Decoration
*6 Chocolate Butterflies**

Add beaten condensed milk to the ice cream instead
of cream. Melt butter and sugar in a saucepan. Add
bread crumbs and stir over medium heat until the
bread crumbs are crisp and golden. Drain, cool and
chill.

Beat the bread crumbs and Tia Maria into the ice
cream with final beating.

Serve in liqueur glasses, and decorate each
portion with a Chocolate Butterfly.

Chocolate Chip and Raisin

¾ pint; 6 portions

2 tablespoons raisins
2 tablespoons dark rum
2 ounces semi-sweet chocolate
½ quantity Vanilla Ice Cream recipe

To serve
6 Duet cookies (page 69)

Place raisins and rum in a small bowl and leave
several hours.

Finely chop the chocolate and fold into the ice
cream with the raisins after the final beating.

Finish as for basic recipe.

Serve tiny scoops in glasses, with Duet cookies.

To freeze successfully
For best results, freeze ice creams in a
shallow, metal container.

Iced Gâteaux

Differently flavored and textured ice creams and sorbets can be combined to
create exotic desserts, mixed and matched in a variety of shapes.

Cassata Roll

One 4½in roll, 3in in diameter; 8 portions

1 quantity Cassata Ice Cream (opposite)
12 tablespoons marzipan
A few drops green food coloring

Decoration
2 tablespoons whipped cream
A few walnut halves

Place Cassata Ice Cream in a 1¾ cup empty food
can. Freeze.

Unmold the ice cream by opening the other end
of the can and holding it in your hands for a few
minutes before pushing out.

Knead the marzipan with a little food coloring
until evenly colored. Roll out and trim to 4½ ×
11in. Place roll on the marzipan and roll up, putting
seam underneath.

Wrap in plastic wrap. Place in the freezer until
required.

Pipe cream along the top and decorate with
walnut halves.

Slice the roll and serve.

Iced Layered Gâteau

One 6 × 3in gâteau; 6 portions

¹/₂ quantity Vanilla Ice Cream recipe (page 136)
4 ounces dark chocolate, grated
2 tablespoons dark rum
2 teaspoons instant coffee
One 6 × 3in thin Chocolate Oblong*
Sixteen 1¹/₂in thin Chocolate
*   Triangles**
Knob of butter
1 cup whipping cream

Follow the basic recipe for Vanilla Ice Cream up to the stage where the custard thickens. Divide the hot custard mixture between two bowls. Stir 4 ounces chocolate into one and when melted beat in the rum. Stir the coffee into the other bowl.

Leave both custards to cool, stirring occasionally. Cover and chill.

Whip the cream from the basic recipe until it forms soft peaks, divide between the bowls and fold in. Place bowls in the freezer for 1 hour, beating twice.

Line two pans or containers, each with a 6 × 3in base, with a strip of foil measuring about 12 × 3in. After the final beating, pour the ice cream into separate pans, reserve 1 tablespoon of chocolate ice cream for decoration, and return to the freezer for 1 hour.

To Assemble Gâteau

Place Chocolate Oblong on a freezer-proof plate or board. Turn out coffee ice cream and place on top. Repeat with chocolate ice cream. Return to freezer.

Whip cream until stiff, spread over the top and around the sides. Streak in the reserved chocolate ice cream over the top. Decorate the sides with Chocolate Triangles and return the gâteau to the freezer.

Place gâteau in the refrigerator for 30 minutes to soften slightly before serving.

Iced Bombe

Two 1 pint bombes; 12 portions

¹/₂ quantity Vanilla Ice Cream (page 136)
2 tablespoons brandy
A few drops yellow food coloring
¹/₂ quantity Red Cherry Ice Cream (page 132)

Decoration
3 tablespoons whipped cream

Place two 1³/₄ cup metal molds in the freezer. Soften the Vanilla Ice Cream and beat in the brandy and a few drops of food coloring to tint yellow. Return ice cream to the freezer until firm but not hard.

Using two-thirds of the Vanilla Ice Cream, spread it thickly around the inside of each mold leaving a suitable space in the center for filling. Return the molds to the freezer.

Part freeze the Red Cherry Ice Cream and pack into the centers of the molds. Level the top and re-freeze.

Spread the reserved Vanilla Ice Cream across the base of each bombe. Cover with foil and return to the freezer until ready to use.

Unmold the bombe by wrapping a dish towel, wrung out in hot water, around the mold for a few seconds. Tap mold firmly to release the bombe. Place bombe on a chilled serving plate and put in the refrigerator.

Place cream in a piping bag fitted with a small star tube and use to decorate the bombe. Place in the refrigerator up to 10 minutes before serving or replace in the freezer.

> Ingredients, sauces, edible containers, etc that are asterisked in the recipes on these pages are given in detail on pages 147 to 156. For exact page numbers, refer to the index at the end of the book

Right, from top *Cassata Roll (page 137); 6 × 3in Iced Layered Gâteau (this page); Iced Bombe (this page).*

Water Ices, Granitas, Sorbets

Make water ices from juicy citrus fruits and wines and liqueurs to give them a tangy taste. Granitas are perfect for hot days; their tiny crystals are especially refreshing. Serve in tiny chilled glasses, on their own or with fruit purée, liqueur or champagne poured over. Sorbets are strongly flavored ices made from meringue and fruit purée, and are easy to make because they do not need to be beaten during freezing.

Water Ice

This recipe is suitable for citrus and other juicy fruits, wines and liqueurs.

1 pint; 8 portions

1 cup water
½ cup sugar
Flavoring (see following recipes)
1 egg white

Place water and sugar in a heavy-based saucepan. Heat gently until the sugar has dissolved, then increase heat and boil rapidly for 2 minutes.

Remove syrup from heat, pour into a bowl and stir occasionally until cool. Add flavoring, chill for ½ hour, pour into a large metal bowl, cover with foil and freeze for about 1 hour until the mixture is frozen ½ inch in from the sides. Remove from the freezer and beat until mushy or quickly mix in a food processor.

Beat egg whites until they form soft peaks. Fold into the iced mixture and return to the freezer for 3 hours, stirring at hourly intervals. Cover and freeze until firm. Place water ice in the refrigerator for 30 minutes before serving.

Passion Fruit Water Ice

¾ pint; 6 portions

½ quantity Water Ice recipe
3 passion fruits

Decoration
6 Chocolate Hearts*

Halve the passion fruits, scoop out the flesh into a strainer placed over a measuring jug. Stir flesh and leave to drain for 15 minutes, stirring occasionally until only seeds remain in the strainer. Make the juice up to ⅝ cup with water. Stir into the cooled syrup. Finish as in the basic Water Ice recipe.

Decorate each portion with a Chocolate Heart.

Fruit Sorbets

Suitable fruits are raspberries, strawberries, loganberries, gooseberries, blackberries, apples, pears, peaches, nectarines, apricots, black currants, red currants, damsons, plums, greengages, melon, mango, mangosteen, kiwi fruit and mixtures of these fruits.

1 pint; 8 portions

1 cup prepared fruit
½ cup sugar
2 egg whites
½ cup superfine sugar

Cook the fruit, if necessary, adding water or wine to moisten, but keeping the fruit concentrated, and strain if desired.

Add sugar to the fruit and leave to cool, then chill well.

Beat the egg whites until stiff; gradually beat in the superfine sugar, then the purée, a little at a time. Place in a shallow freezer container, cover with foil and freeze.

Place in the refrigerator for 15 minutes before serving.

Scoop out the sorbet from the container and place in small chilled dishes or serve in wine glasses topped up with champagne.

Successful sorbets
It is important to chill the fruit purée mixture before beating in the egg white and sugar, and to freeze the sorbet in a shallow container. This will help the mixture freeze smoothly.

Lemon Water Ice

¾ pint; 6 portions

½ quantity Water Ice recipe
3 small lemons
A little white wine or water (if necessary)

Decoration
Strips of lemon peel

Grate the rinds of 2 lemons and add to the sugar syrup before boiling.

Squeeze the juice from all of the lemons, measure and make up to ⅝ cup with wine or water (if necessary). Add to the syrup, strain, cool, chill and then part-freeze as described, and continue with the basic recipe.

Decorate each portion with a twist of lemon peel.

Granita de Menthe

¾ pint; 6 portions

½ quantity Water Ice recipe,
*   omitting egg white*
Juice of 1 lime
½ cup white wine

To serve
6 tablespoons crème de menthe

Make syrup as in basic Water Ice recipe. Measure lime juice and make up to ⅝ cup with the wine. Stir into the cooled syrup and place in a large-based metal freezer container. Freeze until just beginning to set on the base and around the edge. Stir with a metal spoon and shave the ice to form granules. Re-freeze and repeat until the consistency is like crushed ice. Scrape off the granules into chilled small long-stemmed glasses. Pour 1 tablespoon crème de menthe over each portion.

Orange Water Ice

¾ pint; 6 portions

½ quantity Water Ice recipe
2 large oranges
A little white wine or water (if necessary)

To serve
6 tiny lime or pineapple wedges

Make as for Lemon Water Ice, boiling the grated rind of 1 orange with the sugar syrup.

Serve with lime or pineapple wedges.

Coffee Liqueur Granita

1 pint; 10 portions

½ quantity Water Ice recipe, omitting egg white and
*   replacing the sugar with granulated brown sugar*
1 cup strong freshly brewed black coffee
2 tablespoons chocolate liqueur or Tia Maria

To serve
⅝ cup whipped cream or Bailey's Irish Cream
*   Liqueur*
10 chocolate coffee bean candies

Make the basic syrup from the Water Ice recipe using brown sugar instead of white. Add the coffee and leave to cool. Part-freeze, then stir in the liqueur.

Repeat freezing and stirring as for Granita de Menthe until the ice granules resemble shaved ice. Cover and freeze until required.

To serve, scrape off the granules and place in small chilled glasses.

Serve each with a little whipped cream topped with a chocolate coffee bean, or liqueur poured over.

Gifts

A selection of tiny, delicious desserts is the perfect present on any occasion. One of the pleasures of creating individual recipes is the chance to match the gift to the recipient, and of course to the reason – and the season.

What to Make

For a chocolate loving friend's winter birthday, put together an assortment of white Chocolate Cases holding Chantilly Cream, topped by miniature red marzipan berries. An over-worked mother with a job and three children would surely appreciate an icing message piped on a row of cookies, promising a treat a month throughout the year. A summer wedding provides the opportunity for decorative "bouquets" of tiny pink cakes as centerpieces for every table, each plate wreathed with real flowers.

Here are a few more hints on choosing just the right kinds of desserts and presenting them as imaginatively as possible.

Unless you are sure that your present will be used immediately, choose recipes that will stay fresh, or can easily be refrigerated or, even better, frozen. The desserts can then be enjoyed over weeks rather than days. Butter cream will be better than fresh cream for fillings; pieces of candied or preserved fruit make long lasting decorations, more suitable in the circumstances than fresh fruit.

Pastries and cookies are probably safer to transport than gelatins or creams. However, it is possible to give even molded desserts – with the right kind of protective packaging. Individual portions can sometimes be refrigerated or frozen, ready to serve up to three months later.

Presentation

Presentation is one of the most important aspects of making gifts. The wrappings should reflect the occasion, complement the desserts and make it easy to carry the present safely without upsetting the contents.

Make a habit – which can become a fruitful hobby – of collecting small containers. Look for wide-necked jars which can hold fragile decorations like Frosted Flowers and Chocolate Shapes; you won't necessarily need the lids because you can use plastic wrap under covers specially made from gift paper or fabric.

Glass, either clear or colored, always looks wonderful – make sure it is scrupulously clean and sparkling before you put anything inside. Fill some pretty, tall, narrow vases with layers of Frosted Petals in a variety of colors, or tiny Meringue Stars and silver balls.

Antique stalls and junk shops are good hunting grounds for cheap and attractive pieces of glass. Remember to make use of colors and themes by putting Frosted or Fondant Grapes into a green glass, Strawberry Cushions into a pink bowl or, for contrast, whirls of white meringue in a black glass cigarette box.

Unusual boxes are a real find – don't worry too much about their condition or surface, provided they are not irretrievably rusty or covered with grime that won't wash off. You can paint them, or paper them with wrapping paper or the kind of patterned paper that is used for walls in dolls' houses – it comes in tiny brick and trellis designs which are perfect for small desserts.

Flat-bottomed boxes can be shallow or deep. Shallow ones will usually take one layer of tiny desserts; if you use a deep box that will take two layers, adjust the recipes and decorations so that the cakes or macaroons on the bottom have flattish tops that won't be harmed by the stiff paper between the layers.

Don't be put off if you don't like colors or patterns on the containers – spray paints are quick and cheerful and plenty of pretty stencil designs are available if you really want to go to town; making the most of containers can become as much fun as making the desserts.

Think, too, about all kinds of unusual containers. Use decorative coasters as miniature trays to present individual cakes. Fill sake cups from a Japanese souvenir shop with puddings, and stand them in a lacquer-painted cardboard box. A wire stationery tray is a marvelous container for a generous present of cakes or cookies; it is simple to spray it in enamel to complement the desserts, and, of course, it can be used later. Straw cheese platters are perfect for an assortment of cheesecakes. The sections of a

cutlery tray can be filled with Lady Fingers, Cinnamon Doughnuts and Coffee Kisses.

Garden shops are an endless source of suitable containers. Plastic drip trays can be sprayed and decorated, while ceramic ones are particularly fresh and bright in white and pastel colors. Flower pots come in so many sizes that there are usually one or two possibilities for each dessert.

Keep highly decorated novelties separate and protected in small, divided trays intended for growing seedlings. Support them on crumpled, colored foil. For a particularly lavish present, make pretty paper "seed package" signs for a window-box drip tray of desserts and tape them onto the edge at intervals as if it was a miniature seed garden.

Fruit trays in thin wood are appropriate for Apple Strudels or Berry Tartlets. Varnish the wood for extra appeal and tie a bandanna around one corner. Simple baking sheets are inexpensive, especially in bright, old fashioned tin. Make the most of the glitter and decorate the trays with Mexican stencil designs leaving plenty of bare metal to shine through. The rims of the sheets should keep the desserts from sliding off, and you can make a crisscross handle in rope. Pierce holes through the base at each corner, and thread the rope through, knotting it at the top to keep it secure.

Other people's hobbies may be the inspiration for a container. A yachting enthusiast would appreciate a toy boat crammed with "life savers" of tiny ring doughnuts. An ardent gardener should enjoy a lawn of artificial grass covered with a scattering of Cinnamon Flowers. A gourmet would appreciate some of the more difficult-to-make miniatures: tiny Lime Baskets, Chocolate-Coated Strawberries and a jar of Damson Compote with Armagnac.

You can also combine desserts with more practical presents: a jar of prepared fruit and a miniature bottle of complementary liqueur with a flambé dish, or tiny soufflés (and a jar of fruit sauce to serve with them) with a set of individual souffle dishes. Both of these are only for people who will be able to use the ingredients quickly, but a tall glass jar filled with Prunes in Port, Pears with Gin and Lime Juice or Cherries in Red Wine will keep in the refrigerator for a few weeks.

Make an attractive label, to complement the packaging, and also include instructions for use, and a "use by" date. Make edible Lebkuchen labels by cutting the dough into oblongs then placing them on a baking sheet and making a hole, with a skewer, ½ inch from one end, in the center of the cookie. Press out the hole again after baking. When cold, pipe a decorative border in royal icing and, using a paper piping bag filled with a fine writing tube, write the recipient's name in icing. Thread ribbon through the hole and tie it onto the present.

Special Occasions

A new neighbor who has not had time to prepare any food would welcome an appropriate gift from your kitchen: a copy of the local newspaper wrapped around a foil container of Danish Pastries: Stars, Tivolis, Spandauers and Pinwheels.

Festive occasions are, of course, the best times for pulling out all the stops. Fill a ring mold with Christmas Puddings and decorate each with a tiny holly leaf and white icing. Make traditional Lebkuchen Stars and Hearts and hang them on a miniature Christmas tree. Pack an assortment of Mince Pies onto a turkey platter and hold them in place with plastic wrap tied with feather-patterned ribbons. Miniature Crèmes à la Coeur make an edible Valentine card for February 14, while, for Easter, tiny meringues pack nicely into a gold foil Easter egg.

Finally, what about an assortment of finishing touches for a friend who is also an enthusiastic cook? Frosted Rose Petals or Mint Leaves, Chocolate Butterflies and Leaves, Meringue Stars and Glazed Lemon Peel Strands will all help to transform cakes and meringues, creams and gelatins, fritters and crêpes into miniature desserts.

Creating Miniature Desserts

Sauces, creams, icings and other accompaniments and decorations can be inventively combined to create desserts that are as good to look at as they are to eat. This chapter includes basic recipes and also information about how to make – and apply – finishing touches to the desserts.

Basic Recipes

Apricot Glaze

Use to coat cakes and pastries before covering with Quick Fondant Icing, or to coat fruit in tarts.

1 cup apricot jam
Juice of 1 lemon
2 tablespoons water

Place the jam, lemon juice and water in a saucepan. Stir over a low heat until the jam melts, then cook for 1 minute. Press through a nylon strainer and store in a covered jar. To use, warm the glaze and brush over the cake or fruit.

Butters

Brandy Butter

4 tablespoons unsalted butter, softened
1/4 cup sugar
4 tablespoons brandy

Beat butter and sugar together with an electric beater, if possible, until they are pale and fluffy. Add the brandy a few drops at a time, beating continuously until the mixture is light and fluffy.
   Pile into a small dish and serve chilled.

Rum Butter

Make as for Brandy Butter, replacing the sugar with soft dark brown sugar and the brandy with dark rum. Beat in 1/4 teaspoon ground cinnamon.

Creams

Diplomat Cream

1 1/4 cup

Traditionally used in patisserie as a filling, this cream can be flavored and used in many of the same ways as whipped cream. It has more taste, but is less rich.

1 tablespoon custard powder
2 teaspoons Vanilla Sugar
   (page 151)
5/8 cup milk
5/8 cup heavy cream

Blend custard powder and sugar with milk in a saucepan. Bring to a boil stirring and cook for 1 minute. Pour into a small bowl and cover the surface with plastic wrap to keep a skin from forming. Leave until cold then chill.
   Beat the cream until thick. Gradually beat in the custard and any flavoring.

Flavorings
Liqueur
Add 3 tablespoons of liqueur, brandy or rum.

Fruit
Add the finely grated rind of a small orange or lemon.

Coffee
Add 1 tablespoon instant coffee with the milk.

Chocolate
Add 2 ounces grated semi-sweet chocolate to the hot cooked custard.

Left *Selection of decorations for miniature desserts.*

Pastry Cream (Crème Patissière)

Also called French Pastry Cream and Confectioner's Custard. Use this filling for pastries, cakes and tarts.

¼ cup

1¼ cup milk
1 vanilla bean
2 egg yolks
¼ cup sugar
2 tablespoons all-purpose flour

Place the milk and vanilla bean in a small saucepan and bring slowly to a boil. Beat the egg yolks and sugar together until thick, then beat in the flour. Strain a little of the milk into the egg mixture then add the remainder, beating all the time. Return the mixture to the saucepan and bring slowly to a boil, beating continuously. Cook about 1 minute then pour into a bowl and cover the surface with plastic wrap to keep a skin from forming. Cool then chill until required.

Rich Butter Cream

Use this cream to fill cakes and to decorate cookies and pastries. Cover closely with plastic wrap before storing in the refrigerator.

¼ cup sugar
1 egg yolk
10 tablespoons unsalted butter

Place 6 tablespoons water in a small saucepan with the sugar. Stir over a low heat until the sugar has dissolved then boil for about 5 minutes until the syrup registers 220°F, the thread stage, on a sugar thermometer. To test, dip a teaspoon in the syrup, cool slightly, then press another spoon into the syrup on the back of the spoon. Pull the spoons apart: If a thread forms, the syrup is ready.

Beat the egg yolk in a small bowl and gradually beat in the sugar syrup to make a soft mousse. Continue beating until it is cold. Beat the butter until soft, then gradually beat in the egg mousse a little at a time. Flavor as below.

Vanilla
Use Vanilla Sugar (page 151) or add a few drops of vanilla extract.

Lemon, Orange or Lime
Add 1 teaspoon finely grated rind and 1 tablespoon juice.

Chocolate
Add 1 ounce grated semi-sweet chocolate to the egg yolk with the hot syrup.

Coffee
Add 1 teaspoon instant coffee dissolved in 2 teaspoons boiling water.

Praline
Add 2 tablespoons Praline (opposite).

Liqueur
Add 2 tablespoons strongly flavored liqueur.

Green Marzipan

Use a skewer to stab green coloring into a piece of white marzipan, of the size required, then knead the marzipan until smooth and evenly colored.

Icings

Chocolate Fudge Icing

Use to fill and frost cakes and pastries. Cover with plastic wrap and store in the refrigerator until required.

4 ounces semi-sweet chocolate
4 tablespoons butter
1 egg, beaten
¾ cup powdered sugar, sifted

Break up the chocolate and place with the butter in a bowl over a saucepan of hot, but not boiling, water. Stir occasionally until melted then gradually beat in the egg.

Remove the bowl from the heat and beat in the sugar.

Note
Add less powdered sugar if a smooth, flowing icing is required. Add up to ¼ cup more powdered sugar to make a thick icing for swirling on cakes.

Storage
It is often impractical to make small quantities of these standard recipes. Make a "normal" size batch each time, and store in the refrigerator or freezer.

Glacé Icing

Sufficient to coat the top of one 5in cake

⁵⁄₈ cup powdered sugar
1 tablespoon boiling water
1 teaspoon lemon juice
Food coloring, optional

Sift the powdered sugar into a small bowl, add the water and lemon juice and mix to form a thick icing which coats the back of the spoon.

Add food coloring, if desired: dip a skewer into the coloring and shake one drop into the icing. Mix and repeat until the desired color is made.

To use, place the bowl of icing in a saucepan of boiling water and stir gently. Pour or spoon over the cake and spread with the back of the spoon. Leave until set.

Flavourings
Lemon
Replace the boiling water with lemon juice.

Orange
Replace the boiling water with orange juice and the lemon juice with orange flower water.

Coffee
Replace the boiling water and lemon juice with strong black coffee.

Quick Fondant Icing

Use to coat cakes, petits fours, tartlets and cookies and fruits.

1¼ cups powdered sugar
2 to 3 tablespoons warmed Sugar Syrup
(page 150)

Sift the powdered sugar into a bowl and beat in sufficient warm Sugar Syrup until the icing coats the back of the spoon or is the necessary consistency.

Tint with food colorings, if desired, and knead flavorings into the sugar paste.

Note
The icing can be left to set, then stored. To use, chop the set fondant and then put in a cup or bowl in a saucepan of boiling water, with Sugar Syrup. Stir occasionally until the fondant has melted. A ratio of 2 tablespoons fondant to 1 teaspoon syrup gives a good coating consistency.

Royal Icing

1 egg white
³⁄₄ cup powdered sugar

Mix the egg white and powdered sugar until they are the consistency of thick cream, then beat with a wooden spoon until the icing stands in stiff peaks.

Keep the bowl covered with a damp cloth, then use to cover cakes and for piping decorations.

Shiny Chocolate Icing

Sufficient to cover the top and sides of one 5in cake

3 ounces semi-sweet chocolate
2 tablespoons boiling water
1 teaspoon corn oil
1 tablespoon sugar

Break up the chocolate and place with the water, oil and sugar in a small bowl over a saucepan of hot, but not boiling, water. Leave until the chocolate has melted then stir gently to mix.

Pour over the cake or dip cookies and pastries in the icing.

Pink Marzipan

Make as for Green Marzipan (opposite), using pink food coloring.

Praline

Use to flavor Chantilly Cream, Rich Butter Cream and Meringues.

¹⁄₄ cup unblanched almonds
¹⁄₄ cup sugar

Prepare a baking sheet with a light brush of oil. Put the almonds and sugar in a small heavy saucepan and heat slowly until the sugar melts and turns pale golden brown. Gently stir to coat the nuts in caramel and continue cooking until it turns deep golden brown. Quickly turn out onto the oiled baking sheet and leave until cold.

Crush to a fine powder using a pestle and mortar, a rolling pin, or put in an electric blender.

Store in a tightly closed jar for up to three months.

Sugar Syrup

Use to add to chocolate for piping, to mix with liqueur and fruit juices, to soak and moisten cakes and for Quick Fondant Icing (page 149).

1/4 teaspoon cream of tartar
1 cup sugar

Dissolve the cream of tartar in 1 teaspoon water.

Dissolve the sugar in 5/8 cup of water in a small heavy saucepan over a low heat stirring occasionally. Increase the heat and bring to a boil. Add the cream of tartar then boil until the syrup reaches the thread stage of 220°F on a sugar thermometer. To test, dip a teaspoon in the syrup, cool slightly, then press another spoon into the syrup on the back of the spoon. Pull the spoons apart. If a thread forms, the syrup is ready.

Remove from the heat, cool and strain into a jar. The syrup can be stored for up to two months in a jar and does not need refrigerating.

Sauces

Custard Sauce

For speed, follow the directions on a package of custard powder and make to the desired consistency with milk and sugar. For a finer flavor, try this recipe.

4 portions

1 1/8 cups milk
1 vanilla bean
2 egg yolks
1/4 cup sugar
1 teaspoon all-purpose flour

Place the milk and vanilla bean in a small saucepan and bring slowly to a boil.

Meanwhile, cream the yolks, sugar and flour together in a bowl, gradually add the flavored milk, then return to the saucepan and stir over a low heat until the sauce almost boils.

Remove from the heat, take out the vanilla bean and pour the sauce into a serving boat.

Rinse the vanilla bean, leave to dry in a warm place, then re-use.

Fruit Sauce

Follow this recipe when using peaches, apricots, nectarines, plums, damsons, also pineapple.

1 1/8 cup

1 cup prepared fruit
4 tablespoons wine (red for red fruits, white for pale fruits)
1/4 cup sugar
1 tablespoon Armagnac
2 to 3 tablespoons Sugar Syrup (left)

Cook the fruit gently in wine in a small saucepan. Blend and strain if necessary. Return to the saucepan and add sugar, stir over a low heat until dissolved, then boil for 1/2 to 1 minute. Leave to cool then add the Armagnac and adjust the consistency with Sugar Syrup. If desired, use an extra 2 tablespoons chopped fruit, remove with a slotted spoon before blending then return to the sauce after cooling.

Jam Sauce

Use apricot, strawberry, raspberry or plum jam, or orange or lime marmalade.

1 1/8 cup

1/2 cup jam
3 tablespoons lemon or lime juice
6 to 8 tablespoons Sugar Syrup (above left)
2 tablespoons spirit or liqueur

Heat the jam gently in a small pan with the lemon juice and Sugar Syrup and stir until melted. Strain, if necessary, then stir in the liquor or liqueur. Adjust the consistency with more Sugar Syrup, if necessary.

Use brandy or Armagnac for apricot sauce, Cointreau for strawberry sauce, kirsch or kümmel for raspberry sauce, slivowitch with plum jam, whiskey or Drambuie with orange marmalade and white wine with lime marmalade. Add 2 tablespoons chopped ginger to marmalade sauces.

Soft-Fruit Sauce

This recipe is suitable for raspberries, loganberries, blackberries, mulberries, cranberries and strawberries.

1 ⅛ cup

1 cup fruit
¼ cup sugar
2 to 3 tablespoons Sugar Syrup (far left)
1 tablespoon liqueur (optional)

Place fruit in a small saucepan and heat until the juice runs. Add the sugar and stir to dissolve. Bring to a boil and cook quickly for about ½ minute. Strain and cool. Add Sugar Syrup and liqueur to reach the required consistency.

Use kirsch for raspberries and loganberries, Grand Marnier for strawberries, mulberries and loganberries, port for cranberries and crème de cassis for blackberries. Add 2 tablespoons whole fruit just before serving, if desired.

To freeze fruit sauces
Pour the sauce into ice-cube trays or small ¼ cup containers. Pack in plastic bags, seal and freeze. To thaw, heat gently for serving hot; thaw at room temperature for serving cold.

Hot Chocolate Sauce

About ⅝ cup

4 ounces semi-sweet chocolate,
  chopped
2 tablespoons powdered sugar
1 tablespoon unsalted butter,
  chopped

Place all the ingredients in a bowl with ¼ cup hot water and place over a pan of hot water.
   Heat until the chocolate has melted, stir well and serve hot or warm.

Vanilla Sugar

Make this for flavoring ice creams, cakes, Chantilly Cream and sweet pastry.

2 vanilla beans
1 cup sugar

Cut up the vanilla beans into four or five pieces and bury in the sugar in a jar. Cover securely and store in the cupboard for two days to allow the flavor to penetrate the sugar.
   The sugar will keep for up to a year before the flavor fades.

Finishing Touches

Chocolate Decorations

Various types of chocolate are available and it is important to choose the right one.
   Semi-sweet bar chocolate, also called couverture, has the best flavor and should be used when flavoring desserts or in decorations where there is a considerable amount of chocolate. The disadvantage of this type of chocolate is that it will not set after melting unless it is first "tempered". This involves heating, cooling and stirring the chocolate to make the two different crystals in cocoa butter compatible before the chocolate is cooled to the working temperature of 88°F for dark chocolate and 87°F for milk chocolate and white chocolate.

To temper chocolate

Use a minimum of 10 ounces. Chop two-thirds and grate the remainder. Place the chopped chocolate in a small saucepan or bowl that will completely fit over another saucepan, leaving no space for steam to spoil the chocolate (or into a double boiler). Pour some hot but not boiling water into the lower saucepan and melt the chopped chocolate above it away from the heat, stirring occasionally. The top saucepan or bowl must not touch the water and must just feel warm. Place a thermometer in the chocolate and remove the bowl from the heat when the temperature registers 100°F. The lumps may not all be melted. Dry the bottom of the pan or bowl then add the grated chocolate. Give it a good stir then heat it up to 88°F, stirring all the time until it becomes smooth. Try not to beat in any air. Leave for 5 minutes off the heat, stir, then reheat and keep at 88°F. To see if it has tempered, dip a dry, cold knife in the chocolate. It should set hard on the knife and crack when broken off.

Chocolate Cases

Use small paper cake cases, dariole molds, brioche or patty pans, cream horn pans, etc.

If using non-metal containers, cover them in a layer of plastic wrap to ensure easy removal of the chocolate case.

For 6 Chocolate Cases, use 3 ounces chocolate. With a small brush paint the *inside* of the paper cases, brioche or patty pans and dariole molds with a layer of tempered dark, milk or white chocolate. Paint the *outside* of cream horn pans with chocolate. Invert onto waxed paper and leave the chocolate to set. Repeat until three layers of chocolate have been completed. Leave to set hard in refrigerator, then carefully slip the chocolate case from the pan.

Chocolate Shells
Use tiny scallop shells covered with a layer of plastic wrap. Paint the outside of the shells. Pry the chocolate from the shells when set, and ease away the plastic wrap.

For larger quantities
Use extra chocolate and fill the metal cases to the brim with melted chocolate, pour away excess and leave to set upside down on a wire rack.

Chocolate Curls

Spread tempered dark, milk or white chocolate on a cold surface and leave until almost hard. Using a sharp, straight bladed knife, draw the knife at a 45° angle across the chocolate, shaving off a curl. Leave the curls to harden in the refrigerator. Alternately, use a potato peeler or knife to shave off the flat side of a chocolate bar.

Chocolate Flakes

Prepare dark, milk or white chocolate as for Chocolate Curls, then simply scrape off flakes of chocolate, over a piece of non-stick baking parchment, or grate the chocolate directly over the dessert or gâteau.

Chocolate Hearts

Spread tempered dark, milk or white chocolate thinly over a piece of smooth non-stick baking parchment or waxed paper. Leave until chocolate is dry but not hard. Using small, heart-shaped cookie cutters, cut out shapes. Slide paper onto a baking sheet and place in the refrigerator to harden the chocolate. Peel away the parchment or paper and store in a small container in the refrigerator.

Chocolate Leaves

Wash and dry small leaves. Using a fine paint brush, lightly coat the underside of the leaves with tempered dark, milk or white chocolate. Leave to dry, chocolate side uppermost, on waxed paper or non-stick baking parchment. Place in the refrigerator to set. Carefully peel off the leaves and store in small containers in the refrigerator.

Chocolate Rolls

Spread tempered chocolate thinly over a marble slab or clean surface. When dry, but not hard, make rolls by pushing (or pulling) a long bladed straight-edged knife held at a slight angle across the top of the chocolate to make thin rolls. Store in a small box in the refrigerator.

Chocolate Shapes

Spread tempered dark, milk or white chocolate thinly over waxed paper or smooth non-stick baking parchment. Leave until the chocolate is dry but not hard, then cut out shapes using small cookie cutters. Slide paper onto a baking sheet and leave in the refrigerator while it hardens. Peel away the paper or parchment and store the shapes in a small box in the refrigerator.

Geometric shapes: squares, triangles, wedges

Use about 3 ounces tempered chocolate for sixteen 1½in squares or 32 triangles or 24 wedges.

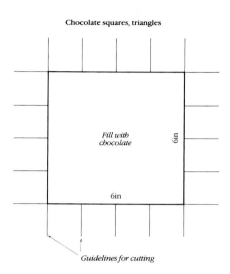

Chocolate squares, triangles

Fill with chocolate

6in

6in

Guidelines for cutting

On a smooth piece of non-stick baking parchment draw a 6in square. Mark along each side at 1½in intervals and draw lines outwards at right-angles. Alternately, draw three 5in circles and divide each into 8 equal wedges. Extend the lines beyond the circle or square. Turn the parchment over and place on a flat surface. Secure this firmly to the surface using tape or thumb tacks.

Spread melted chocolate evenly over the parchment within the marked lines. Leave the chocolate to dry.

With a straight bladed knife cut the chocolate into squares or wedge-shaped portions using the extended lines as a guide. Cut the squares diagonally to make triangles. Chill and store in the refrigerator, in a small container.

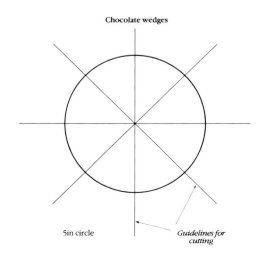

Chocolate wedges

5in circle

Guidelines for cutting

Oblongs

To make an oblong, use about 2 ounces chocolate and draw a 6 × 3in oblong on the baking parchment, then continue as above.

Note

The size of the basic shape on the paper, and of squares, triangles, etc can be altered for different recipes. For example, for twenty-five 1in squares, draw a 5in square.

To Pipe Chocolate

Use Piping Chocolate to decorate cakes, etc or for various motifs. White chocolate can be colored for extra effect. Color as for Quick Fondant Icing (page 149) but use powdered colorings.

Draw shapes on a smooth piece of non-stick baking parchment. Reverse the parchment and secure with tape or thumb tacks.

Paper Piping Bag

Suitable paper
Non-stick baking parchment
Waxed paper

Cut a piece of paper 10 × 8in (A). Fold and cut in half diagonally to make two triangles each with a blunt corner (B).

Hold the middle of the long side of one of the triangles with the left hand and with your right hand fold the blunt corner Y around in front to just below point X, to form a cone (C).

Holding the pointed end of the cone in the left hand, twist corner Z round the cone and up behind cone to corner X (D).

Fold the extra paper at the top down twice to secure the cone (E).

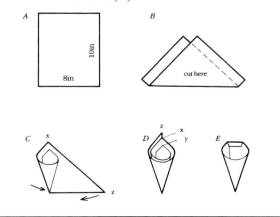

Piping Chocolate

4 ounces chocolate
2 tablespoons powdered sugar
A few drops of water

Melt the chocolate and stir in the powdered sugar. Add a few drops of water to give a thick piping consistency, which should fall heavily from the spoon. Alternately, for large quantities, beat in Sugar Syrup (page 150) until the required consistency is reached.

Place the chocolate in a small paper icing bag (page 153). Fold over the top and snip off the end to the thickness of the piping required and gently squeeze out the chocolate around the shapes, holding the bag about 1in above the paper.

Leave until the chocolate is dry but not hard, then store in a small box in the refrigerator.

Always pipe extra shapes or motifs to allow for breakages.

Chocolate Butterflies

With Raised Wings

After drawing the shape on non-stick baking parchment, using dark Piping Chocolate, pipe a line around the edge of each wing. Still using a piping bag, fill the center of each wing with chocolate. Leave to dry, then peel off the paper.

Pipe a thick line of white chocolate about ½in long onto baking parchment or waxed paper. Arrange wings standing up on each side. Support them with small rolls made from paper towels and leave until the chocolate has set. Pipe antennae when completely dry; carefully peel off the paper. Store in a small box in the refrigerator.

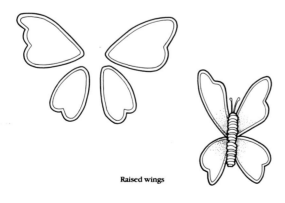

Raised wings

Flat Butterfly

Pipe wings as described. When dry, pipe a thick line of chocolate down the center with added antennae.

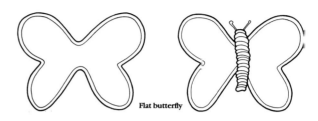

Flat butterfly

Pink Chocolate Butterfly

Proceed as for the variations above, but fill the center of each wing with white chocolate to which powdered pink coloring has been added. See Quick Fondant Icing (page 149) for method.

Chocolate Motifs

Pipe a line from A to B, then in a clockwise direction pipe oval shapes increasing in size but keeping the bases at the same point.

Colored Crystals

Sprinkle these crystals over meringues before baking, or over glacé iced cakes and cookies and whipped cream immediately before serving.

2 rounded tablespoons sugar
A few drops of food coloring

Place the sugar and 2 or 3 drops of food coloring in a small bowl. Using a small palette knife, work the crystals against each other until the sugar is evenly colored. Spread the sugar over a piece of waxed paper or non-stick baking parchment and leave to dry in a warm place.

Store in a dry, screwtop jar.

Frosted Leaves, Flowers

Suitable flowers are flat, thin-petalled flowers such as roses (not Christmas roses), primroses, pansies, sweet peas, nasturtiums, forget-me-nots, lilac and violets, also fruit blossoms such as apple, pear and cherry. Individual petals, such as rose petals, can also be frosted.

Suitable leaves are rose, mint, sage, thyme, lemon balm, Italian parsley, lamb's tongue.

Note
Some flowers, including bulb flowers, are inedible so if in doubt, remove before eating the dessert.

1 egg white
2 teaspoons water
Superfine sugar, to coat

Prepare the items to be frosted. Pick flowers and leaves just before using.

Flowers
Shake lightly upside down then spread out on paper towels and leave 15 minutes (to encourage any insects to crawl out).

Leaves
Gently wash and dry leaves on paper towels. Spread out to dry thoroughly. Avoid bruising leaves.

Place egg white and water in a small bowl and beat together until the egg white is no longer stringy but not too frothy. Using a fine paint brush, paint the under and top side of the petals or leaves with a thin layer of egg white, making sure they are evenly yet not thickly coated. Sprinkle lightly with sugar.

Spread the frosted items on waxed paper or non-stick baking parchment and leave to dry in an airy place but away from direct sunlight which would bleach the color. Store between sheets of tissue paper for up to four weeks for leaves, two weeks for flowers.

Note
Some flowers will darken or go limp if their petals are bruised or if the flowers are not at their peak when picked. Discard these. It is sensible to frost more flowers than are needed because they are very fragile.

Glazed Citrus Peel Strands

Suitable fruits are oranges, lemons, limes, grapefruit. Choose firm fruit with a good color and a rough skin.

1 orange or 1 lemon or 2 limes
³⁄₈ cup water
¹⁄₄ cup sugar

Scrub fruit with a small brush under running water. Using a potato peeler or small vegetable knife shave off long strips of peel down the length of the fruit, avoiding the white pith. Place the peel on a chopping board and cut into thin strips with a sharp knife.

Place the water in a small saucepan and bring to a boil. Add the peel, reduce heat, cover and simmer for 1 or 2 minutes until the peel is tender. Remove with a slotted spoon. Add the sugar to the pan and stir until dissolved. Increase the heat and cook rapidly until the syrup is reduced by half. Return the peel to the pan and continue cooking uncovered, stirring occasionally, until well glazed. Remove the peel and gently shake off any excess syrup. Leave the peel on non-stick baking parchment or waxed paper to cool. When cold, store in a small jar or box between pieces of waxed paper.

To glaze fruit slices
Small slices of oranges, lemons, limes and kumquats can be glazed as above.

Marzipan Cut-outs

Flowers

Six 1¹⁄₂in flowers

³⁄₄–1 cup Green Marzipan (page 148)
Powdered sugar

Roll out Green Marzipan and trim to 4 × 14in. Cut down its length into three 1¹⁄₄in strips, then cut twelve 1¹⁄₄in leaf shapes diagonally from each strip. Sprinkle six individual tartlet pans with powdered sugar and press six leaves, slightly overlapping, into each. Leave several hours, until the marzipan has set, then remove from the pans and leave to dry overnight.

Leaves

About 24 leaves

¼ cup Green Marzipan (page 148)
Powdered sugar
Melted chocolate

Lightly dust work surface with sifted powdered sugar. Knead marzipan until smooth, then roll out to ⅛in thick. Use a leaf shaped cutter to cut out as many shapes as possible. Lift leaves from the work surface with a small scapula and place them on waxed paper or non-stick baking parchment. Mark veins with a knife before leaving to dry. To curve leaves, place them over the handles of wooden spoons.

To decorate, brush melted chocolate over half or the complete top surface of each leaf, or pipe a thin line of chocolate down the center to represent a vein. Store between layers of waxed paper or baking parchment in a cardboard box.

Note

If no cutters are available, roll out the marzipan and cut into ¾in strips. Cut each strip diagonally at ¾in intervals. Shape the edges of each to form a leaf. Lightly mark the veins of the leaf with a pointed knife; leave to dry, then decorate as above.

Hearts, Daisies

¼ cup Pink Marzipan (page 149)
Powdered sugar

Roll out marzipan as for leaves and cut out shapes using a cookie cutter. Alternately, use a small fluted cutter for daisies and a small round plain cutter for hearts and shape edges where necessary. Store as for leaves.

Piped Cream Decorations

Piped cream can be used either as a single star or an elaborate design. Whipped cream freezes well and can also be used on frozen desserts.

Whip any spare cream with a little sugar – about 1 teaspoon to 6 tablespoons heavy cream – and pipe stars or whirls on a baking sheet. Once frozen, these motifs can be stored in a box interleaved with non-stick baking parchment or waxed paper and used as instant decoration.

To whip cream

For best results use a mixture of light and heavy creams, 2 parts heavy to 1 part light, or use whipping cream.

Chill the cream, bowl and balloon or electric beater before using. An electric beater can over-whip the cream and can cause it to separate. Whip quickly at first until the cream has a matt-looking surface, then whip slowly until it stands in soft peaks and does not fall off the upturned beater. When whipped, the cream should have doubled in volume.

To pipe the cream

Piping tends to "frill" the cream, especially if it has been over-whipped, and warmth from your hand can quickly turn it to butter. Whip cream in small batches, and use a clean, cold bag and piping tube. Large nylon piping bags are available with a large plain or star Savoy or potato tube.

Fold the piping bag back on itself about half way down and stand in a cup for easy filling. Place only a few tablespoons of whipped cream in the bag at one time. Pull the top of the piping bag up and fold over to enclose the cream. Press from the top of the bag and avoid cradling the bag in the palm of the hand, which will overheat the cream. If the cream "frills" or separates, wash and dry the bag and start again.

Toasted Nuts

Suitable nuts
Blanched almonds – whole, flaked, chopped
Hazelnuts – whole, chopped
Mixed chopped nuts

Prepare a medium hot broiler. Remove the rack and line the broiler pan with foil. Spread the nuts over the foil and toast until evenly browned, occasionally stirring the nuts and turning them over to ensure even toasting. This will take only a few seconds depending on the quantity of nuts being toasted. Lift the foil out of the pan and leave the nuts to cool. Rub off the hazelnut skins between two paper towels, if necessary.

The cold nuts can be stored for a few days in a screwtop jar, but are best used the same day.

Index

Picture acknowledgments

Edmund Goldspink page 111
David Burch page 2
All other photographs by
David Jordan

Color separations by
Anglia Reproductions